THE
THRONE ROOM
COMPANY

ENDORSEMENTS

Shawn Bolz is the real deal! What he shares in this amazing book are the first fruits of what many will experience in the days ahead.

—CHE AHN, Senior Pastor, Harvest Rock Church

Beloved, this book is radical! A potpourri of wisdom pulled from personal visitations, prophetic revelation, and profound teaching, Shawn Bolz has gathered rare keys of revelation that will redefine how you approach and appreciate God. What lies before you is a holy invitation—to come up higher to where angels fear to tread—to the very throne room of God.

—JILL AUSTIN, Founder, Master Potter Ministries

The Throne Room Company is truly apostolic in nature, giving readers a glorious glimpse into the heavenly realm. Shawn Bolz is one of the fathers of a new breed of prophets and apostles. In this book, he gives a prophetic description of how the Body of Christ will look at the end of the age. I gladly recommend this book!

—TODD BENTLEY, Founder, Fresh Fire Ministries

At a time when our contemporary culture is crying out in hunger for a transcendent reality, *The Throne Room Company* invites us to a dynamic encounter with our heavenly Father. Shawn Bolz's wonderful book offers a passionate partnership with God in His divine purposes on the Earth.

—MIKE BICKLE, Director, International House of Prayer in Kansas City

The Lord has given us a profound invitation to enter into His throne room. Shawn Bolz releases awesome insights so we can better position our hearts for this ascension to God's throne. Your life will be enriched and blessed as you read the thrilling pages of this book.

—BOBBY CONNER, Founder, Eagle's View Ministries

The Throne Room Company is a trumpet call to the Body of Christ. The spiritual insights given to Shawn Bolz will help to unlock the destinies and spiritual opportunities for those desperately hungry to apprehend more of the Lord. As you read this book, may you receive a fresh impartation from Heaven.

—PAUL KEITH AND WANDA DAVIS, Founders, WhiteDove Ministries

There is a new, young generation being given an invitation to "come up here." The Church is going to begin to live out of Heaven, under the government of the Spirit rather than human engineering. This book is that summons, and Shawn Bolz is a prophet for this coming generation.

—LOU ENGLE, President, The Call

The Throne Room Company

Shawn Bolz

STREAMS PUBLISHING HOUSE

P.O. Box 550, North Sutton, New Hampshire 03260

The Throne Room Company
Copyright © 2004 by Shawn Bolz

ISBN: 1-58483-091-3

Creative Director and Managing Editor: Carolyn Blunk
Associate Editor: Jordan Bateman
Contributing Editor: Celeste Pennington
Copy Editor: Dorian Kreindler
Editorial Assistant: Mary Ballotte
Designed by Dan Jamison
Cover design by Mike Bailey

Printed in the United States of America.

FOR A FREE CATALOG
OF STREAMS BOOKS AND OTHER MATERIALS,
CALL 1-888-441-8080 (USA AND CANADA)
OR 603-927-4224

To my family,
who labored toward
my revelation of God's love.

To my parents, Larry and Stacia:
You have been the light of a million fires
that has shown me the way in which to walk.
You have never left your first love, and
it makes my own relationship with
Him burn brighter.

To my sister, Cindy:
You have always been one of my heroes
in the faith. You remind me of the Shulamite
in the Song of Solomon.

To my sister, Jennifer:
You have been the type of friend that defines
the beauty of fellowship.
Thank you for your devotion, even
when I didn't deserve it.

Contents

FOREWORD

IT IS A CLICHÉ WE THROW AROUND ALL THE TIME: "You're known by the company you keep." We use this simple phrase to teach our children to select the right friends. We use it from the pulpit to help foster community in our churches. We use it to guide people away from those with shady reputations.

We use this saying because it holds the truth: We are indeed known by the company we keep! But there is a magnificent spiritual quality to this statement as well. We are known by the company we keep—God. Even more important, however, is that God is known by the company He keeps—us.

Jesus spoke at length about this principle:

> My prayer is not for them alone. I pray also for those who will believe in me through their message, that all of them may be one, Father, just as you are in me and I am in you. May they also be in us so that the world may believe that you have sent me. I have given them the glory that you gave me, that they may be one as we are one: I in them and you in me. May they be brought to complete unity to let the world know that you sent me and have loved them even as you have loved me.
>
> Father, I want those you have given me to be with me where I am, and to see my glory, the glory you have given me because you loved me before the creation of

the world. Righteous Father, though the world does not know you, I know you, and they know that you have sent me. I have made you known to them, and will continue to make you known in order that the love you have for me may be in them and that I myself may be in them.

—JOHN 17:20-26

Jesus was known by His disciples for the company He kept with God the Father. And we are now known by others for the company we keep with Him. What kind of reflection of God are we? Is His light pouring out of us, illuminating the darkness around us? Or have we hid His light under a box, content to hoard the blessing of God? How will God be known to the world if we hide Him from those who need Him most?

I believe *The Throne Room Company* is a key salvo in the battle against darkness. Shawn's experience and teaching should provoke all of us to pursue a deeper intimacy with God than we have ever had. We should be seeking more and more of God's truth, becoming a part of God's throne room company of people who love simply to sit at His feet and be with Him.

This hunger for more intimacy is a hallmark of what God yearns to release on the Earth in the realm of spiritual leadership. In 2002, I had an encounter with the Lord and His Holy Spirit that disintegrated many former opinions I had held. In this encounter the Lord spoke to me and said, "The pecking order in the Church is about to topple. I am going to start promoting unknown people to the fourth row."

To fully understand the gravity of this simple word spoken to me, you must understand what God was referring to about promoting leaders to the fourth row. Several years ago, I had an encounter with a heavenly messenger who took me to the third Heaven. While there, I saw and heard about a great move of God that was coming to the Earth.

Entering an expansive white room, I saw four tiers of pure white rock bleachers on one side of the room. The first three rows were filling up with church leaders. All of the leaders on the third row were very famous, but those leaders on the first two rows I did not know at the time.

The angel looked at me and said, "The key to the next great move of God in the Earth is found in the book of Romans and in particular, chapter four. Contained therein is an unembraced truth that will mark and distinguish this coming move from all other moves of My Spirit."

Suddenly, I understood that each row represented the established pecking order in the Church, and that one day there would be a sudden and great change. The angel told me that one day the Lord would suddenly catapult leaders on the first two rows over those on the third row, who had lorded their ministries over the others. These unknown leaders would then stand on the fourth row, where no one had stood since the early Church.

You see, the Lord does not respect the Church's pecking order. Instead, He respects those with humble hearts and contrite spirits, who are true to Him. It is communion and intimacy that God honors, not works and accomplishments. Humanity has imposed a self-made system of supposed spiritual acknowledgment. If one does not fit into this layered hierarchy (pecking order) and wait to be acknowledged by those above, then one will be shunned for not following human-enforced protocols.

To be truly great in the Kingdom of God, however, we must be humble and passionately in love with the King. Like Mary at Jesus' feet, we need to be content to sit and wait on God. We should hang on His every word. This is what a throne room company does. We must be willing to look foolish in the eyes of our peers, as we proclaim boldly what God has told us to say and do.

It is only through God's power and trust in us that our destiny can be fulfilled. Our own abilities, strategies, and schemes will continually fall short.

In the coming days, God will raise up unknown and humble men and women of faith, who have patiently waited for God to do the miraculous; He will promote them as leaders.

These men and women will be refined by years of making good choices that reflect godly character, ethics, and morality.

These leaders will not be recognized for their titles or ministries, but for the presence of God evidenced in their lives. They will have an intimate and beautiful relationship with their heavenly Father. In addition, many of these will be a company of people who will be taken to God's throne room.

When this happens, supernatural power and miracles will return to the Church. It will not be limited to one person, one church, or one geographic area. God will scatter His manifestations of miraculous power over many cities and nations.

As this thick presence of the Holy Spirit infiltrates the Church, denominational boundaries that have separated churches will become insignificant. A fresh emphasis will be made on having a deeper relationship with the Holy Spirit. People will be known for walking humbly with God as well as with men and women. Past issues that God has permitted to exist will come under greater scrutiny and conviction by the Holy Spirit. A new wave of holiness will fall upon all believers. Repentance from self-righteousness will become a stronger focus. Meekness, which results from sacrificing the right to be right, will be evidenced in the lives of those upon which the Lord's anointing rests.

God will be known by the company He keeps: a gloriously revitalized Church desperately in love with Him. This coming move of the Holy Spirit will not be dependent on a certain individual's gifting or anointing. Rather, the Holy Spirit will sovereignly release this Presence. We simply need to be ready and full of humility, transparency, vulnerability, hunger, and brokenness, so we do not crumple when the weight of God's presence touches us.

The Throne Room Company will help prepare us for this new move of God. We all need to be equipped by emerging leaders like Shawn Bolz, a man with a proven track record of fulfilled prophecy and miraculous healing. Shawn's heart is to disciple and train others, a call he has walked out with the Forerunner School of Ministry in Kansas City and numerous conferences and seminars. Shawn's word to us to pursue intimacy with God is both timely and necessary.

It is my prayer that we would all become a part of the throne room company, relying fully on our intimacy with God to see us through every situation in life. If we are known by the company we keep, then God deserves the greatest company of all.

—John Paul Jackson

Acknowledgments

I WOULD LIKE TO OFFER A SPECIAL THANK YOU TO WhiteDove Ministries: Paul Keith and Wanda Davis, Bob Jones, and the doves! You are such a great ministry family that covers me with the love of Heaven so I can do what I am doing. I am truly and eternally grateful that I am a part of you.

I also want to thank Theresa Lea who helped me know how to believe for Heaven; you are one of the most amazing people I have ever known. I also extend thanks to her family; you have become my family, Byron and Zion.

I am grateful to Jonatan Toledo who has stood faithfully with me year after year, keeping our focus on the highest as we travel the world together. Thank you for being a true "Jonathan" to me.

God bless you Heath King. You are like the little brother that I never had.

To Kadir Raful, you have the biggest servant's heart I have ever known. Thank you for all the deep talks and the gift of your friendship.

I want to extend my most sincere thanks to the Mitchell family. You have loved me with a love that is unnatural to this world; your love has allowed me to press in so much higher. You are some of God's best, and I am humbled to be your friend.

I am also grateful to my friend, Paula Benne. Your prophetic journey has inspired so much of mine. May I grow up to be like you. I can't think of anyone in my life who has understood me the way you have.

Finally, I would like to thank Mike and Diane Bickle and the Kansas City House of Prayer family (especially the night watch). You have inspired so much of my ministry. Your 24/7 devotion has been a dream come true for my life.

CHAPTER ONE

WHEN THE HEAVENS OPEN

*After this I looked, and there before me was a door standing
open in heaven. And the voice I had first heard speaking to me
like a trumpet said, "Come up here, and I will show you what
must take place after this." At once I was in the Spirit, and there
before me was a throne in heaven with someone sitting on it.*

—REVELATION 4:1-2

IN OCTOBER 2002, I WAS TAKEN UP TO HEAVEN TO SEE the throne room of God. It was one of my most profound spiritual experiences.

What I describe to you here is not written in a figurative sense or as a flight of human imagination. One difficulty in describing that spiritual experience, however, lies in my understanding of what I saw. I believe that a supernatural gift of wisdom through the Spirit of Truth is required to make this heavenly experience clear. The other difficulty relates to the difference in the human perception of time and God's eternity.

John the Beloved did such an awesome job of describing what he saw in the book of Revelation. He truly had the Spirit of Wisdom to relate to us what he had seen. Many people consider his language confusing, until they begin to understand how vastly different eternity is. Then, they develop a great respect for this beloved friend of Jesus.

Often people who see into Heaven as it really is cannot clearly communicate what they have seen, unless they have a supernatural gift of wisdom through the Spirit of Truth. Now that I have qualified this concept, I will attempt to present a basic message that came from the greater whole of the experience.

The Radiance of His Glory

When the Heavens opened to me, the atmosphere of Heaven was thick with intense purity in the air. Many spiritual beings surrounded me. An angel guided me into the center of a very large room, which I realized was God's throne room. It had no visible walls; the room seemed as endless as God's awesome presence.

In the center of the room was the glorified Son. His presence was so bright that the pure light coming from His face felt like a walk into the heart of a nuclear explosion. Yet somehow, He gave me grace to be able to walk toward Him.

Although I understood that God dwells in an approachable light, this experience of His glory caused me to become undone.

How can those who are unholy come into the very presence of Holiness without shattering into a million particles? God's very covenant of love was my assurance that I was safe. I held on to it as though it were a contract in my hand, because I was so overwhelmed by the fear of the Lord.

This time I wasn't allowed to get very close. However, just being in such nearness to God was overwhelming. I just stared at Him, the King of all glory. I felt like I was crying out of sheer joy, but no tears fell. It was as if my spirit contained the emotion of weeping but expressed it so much deeper—with a deep sense of astonishment.

Just gazing at God was an act of worship. I didn't have to try and produce words or songs; my whole being was alive in His presence and completely adored Him. It is a natural, automatic response in the midst of His glory.

I was only able to gaze upon Him for a few minutes. I knew if I stayed there much longer, I would not be willing to return to Earth. So, the angel interrupted my sweet communion with Jesus. It was the only time my angelic companion felt awkward. We looked at each other with complete understanding, and then we both obeyed.

Around God's Throne

The angel directed me to look around the throne room. As much as I didn't want to take my eyes off the Lord, I obeyed. Only then, I noticed three groups of people and spirits in the throne room.

The first group seemed to be made up of humans who had passed on into eternity. Somehow I understood these were the saints of old who were still laboring for the purposes of God to come forth on the Earth. Many wore living robes of light that were alive with purpose and embedded with specific markings on them. Some garments seemed so much a part of the person, they appeared to be joined to the person's flesh.

The second group consisted of angels and other heavenly beings. I saw groups of angels who resembled human beings. I also saw a fantastic host of heavenly beings who were flying, floating, running, standing, and lying prostrate. The magnitude of angelic beings God created around Himself was simply stunning. Millions of them were in the throne room. Never before have I been part of such a vast crowd on Earth, and I found it intimidating in the throne room.

Visitors to the Throne Room

Amazingly, the third group was by far the smallest group. It comprised four hundred Christians—mere visitors like myself. These were not people who had passed on to eternity by dying. Instead, they were actual living Christians who were experiencing Heaven at the same time as I, although not everyone realized the fullness of the experience.

Each individual was being led into shafts of light that would fill him or her with revelation about the very heart of Jesus. I knew there was an end-time purpose to each person's visit as well as a divine union with the Lord.

Angels were assigned to each visitor, but not just any angel. Many were angels who had spent thousands of years in the throne room worshipping and communing with Jesus. These angels were sent to carry the atmosphere of the throne room into the very lives of this small company. As I watched these visitors return to Earth, they were literally surrounded by a heavenly atmosphere that came from these angelic assignments. The holiness and glory of the heavenly realm followed them back in token experiences.

These four hundred visitors were getting clear glimpses of Heaven. They were able to see into the mysteries of ages and touch what only a few have touched while living. This group included people of all ages and both sexes. Some in this circle were Christians from the persecuted church, and some were from the Western world. I was surprised to know several by name.

What amazed me most was seeing several children in the group. One was a little boy who was only seven years old. Although it wasn't until I was a late teenager that I had a heavenly experience, I began to see revelation when I was only four years old. Children have the same invitation that we do—to experience the depths of the Holy Spirit's work. In the coming days, I believe that many children on Earth will be invited into a much higher realm of revelation than many of us can imagine.

In the midst of this heavenly scene, I realized that my angelic companion had left me and now the Angel of the Lord was standing near me. He spoke to me about the four hundred Christian visitors:

> "This is the throne room company—those Christians who are called to see and better understand the high calling of eternity, and to bring that message back to the world. What they have seen will set them apart, and it will provoke many to jealousy, yearning for a glimpse."

I knew this experience would set this group apart from other Christians on Earth, not only because of the heavenly revelation, but because of the angels that would be assigned to them from the throne room of God. In addition, they would have tasted the heavenly realm in such a way that would ruin them for anything natural. Encountering this eternal realm would cause a holy and accelerated drive toward it when they returned to Earth.

Even though we numbered only four hundred, the angel said this company would soon multiply; it is the Father's goal to have a whole generation of heavenly minded believers who long for Jesus to return to Earth and claim His reward. Therefore, in our generation an access would be given to encounter Heaven experientially by the Spirit of Revelation.

All of us in the throne room were powerfully drawn into the presence of Jesus Christ. As we looked into this heavenly realm, a supernatural expansion was given to each of us, to carry back the virtue of what we had seen. This virtue of Jesus would bring an expansion that would manifest in each person's character, understanding, relationships, and ministry.

A Season of Visitation

In our generation, various Christians have served as tokens of this heavenly deposit; these ones carried a special anointing or gifting, especially in their love for others. But now, we are entering a targeted season in which a whole generation of people will begin to carry the nature of Jesus Christ on Earth.

What I experienced that October may result in a paradigm shift for many Christians. If a door to Heaven opened to you today, how would that experience affect your passion for Jesus Christ? Or your relationships and daily activities?

In contrast to a life centered around Christian activity, I wonder if all of us might have an ever-increasing desire to walk in the presence of Jesus, in order to carry His mandate both now and into eternity?

For several years, I used to wonder what it would be like if God would give us access to His throne room—to see what the angels see, to know what causes the twenty-four elders and the living creatures to cast down their crowns before the throne. And while I have caught only a glimpse, a whole generation is about to see such things and bring back this heavenly experience in prophecy, music, teaching, business, politics, and in every dimension that will eventually touch the ends of the Earth.

As Christians, one of the most important themes given to us as our heritage is the subject of eternity. Unfortunately, in many respects the message of Heaven has been lost. However, it is clear this will be one of the most prevalent messages in the Body of Christ as we get closer to His return.

Demonic Distractions

Besides our own lack of understanding about eternity and the heavenly realm, we have an enemy who is trying to pervert our understanding of them. Two powerful strategies of the enemy have confounded our perspective.

First, Satan has caused Christians to fear that Heaven's reward is not worth paying the earthly price. This anxiety seems to preoccupy us with our day-to-day human struggles, stealing the focus from God and the greater mandate of our eternal calling.

This spirit of unbelief in our culture comes through a religious spirit, which has always been one of the greatest strongholds of the Church. This religious spirit causes us to be more preoccupied with our struggling humanity, stealing our focus from God. It causes us to become so focused on this temporal life and how we relate to it in our weak attempt at faith that we cannot focus on the greater mandate of our eternal calling.

At the other extreme, the second strategy of the demonic realm is to bring such a narrow focus on end-time eschatology that we miss the true focus of our eternal reward, as our attention is deftly steered onto the bumpy, misunderstood road that leads there. Many of us have missed seeing the true goal of Jesus, even in our pursuit of understanding the end times.

To remain clear of either distraction from the enemy, we need to follow the apostle Paul's example:

> I press on toward the goal to win the prize for which God has called me heavenward in Christ Jesus. All of us who are mature should take such a view of things. And if on some point you think differently, that, too, God will make clear to you.
>
> —PHILIPPIANS 3:14-15

That statement reflects both Paul's calling and his heart's hunger to be with Jesus in Heaven. Both Paul's passion and his witness to the Church—the Body of Christ—grew out of his willingness to become a living testimony of that heavenly call. As a result, Paul did not merely include eternity in his overall blueprint for Christian success, he contended as in a race, pressing on to his eternal call.

This contending for Heaven marked Paul's life and was one of the reasons he was able to call believers to live as he lived. He was not just making himself an example for those called to Church government, and he was not trying to assert that he was the ultimate in Christian virtue either—although his personal integrity was unmatched in his day. No one is without fault. But what Paul gave as a witness to the Body of Christ was his willingness to become a living testimony as one who was completely focused on Jesus in Heaven. Paul's goals were clear, and the price he was willing to pay conveys a truly passionate message to us.

Hell's Secret

Let me give you the secret to hell: The devil resists and even prostitutes the subject of eternity for us, because Satan is jealous of our role in it. Keeping us from eternity is his ultimate goal. In fact, the "father of lies" is disturbed that God would freely give humans what Satan so desired: to be like Jesus, and to be glorified in Heaven with Him.

For this reason Satan works overtime to distract us from who we are and to occupy us in lesser roles. If he can do this to the Church, he will continue to dominate the world, because we have failed to engage in a rightful Kingdom dominion.

For our identity to be fully wrapped up in the Kingdom Age, we must first submit ourselves, including all the lesser roles we perform, to Jesus. When we do this, we can begin to behold Him through the eyes of the Spirit, and we will begin to become like Him in all of His glory even before we enter into the age to come.

Keeping Eternity in Focus

Jesus always used language that pointed to eternity. He longed to be there so much—even while He was on Earth—that Jesus could not separate eternity from His very being. To behold Jesus as He walked the Earth in the flesh was to catch a glimpse of Heaven. He opened up the realms of Heaven through the words He preached, through His miracles, and through His intercession. He revealed an eternity where God—who has no beginning and no end—waits for us in eager anticipation.

God offers us an eternity where we will be a counterpart to

Him. He desires nothing but our affections. He desires that this eternity will be an arena where we will rule and reign with Him—even over angels—having been fully adopted into His inheritance of all creation.

Jesus' life became a sort of "open Heaven." As early Christians considered this teaching, they coined the term "open Heavens." We still pray for this today. Because, when the Heavens open, we will see more fully the object of our desire, the Lord Jesus Christ. Imagine what will happen when a generation begins to carry the atmosphere of Heaven on the Earth.

What we do on the Earth directly relates to our future role in Heaven. For us, Earth is a place where we pay a great price of sacrificing our life here so that we can inherit a much better one in Heaven. Throughout eternity, we will rule and reign with Jesus over all of His creation, as fully adopted sons and daughters of God.

While grace for salvation is free, building a storehouse in Heaven is costly. It will cost us every day, all day long. As we extend ourselves, we run the race here in order to apprehend the prize of Heaven. The apostle Paul illustrates the yearning after this pursuit in his letter to the Philippians:

> I want to know Christ and the power of his resurrec-
> tion and the fellowship of sharing in his sufferings,
> becoming like him in his death, and so, somehow, to
> attain to the resurrection from the dead.
> —Philippians 3:10-11

If we are to pursue the mystery of Jesus in eternity, then we will have to place our eyes upon the goal of Him alone. So many have watered down or limited this very goal, but Jesus lays out that goal for us so clearly:

> …that all of them may be one, Father, just as you are
> in me and I am in you. May they also be in us so that
> the world may believe that you have sent me. I have

given them the glory that you gave me, that they may be one as we are one: I in them and you in me. May they be brought to complete unity to let the world know that you sent me and have loved them even as you have loved me. Father, I want those you have given me to be with me where I am, and to see my glory, the glory you have given me because you loved me before the creation of the world.

—JOHN 17:21-24

Jesus prayed for a divine union with us—His most precious gift. This possibility is almost beyond comprehension. Jesus was tying His destiny to us, in the same way that He tied His destiny to the Father. This is absolutely the most profound idea in the Bible.

Jesus prayed for us to commune fully with the Father and to see Him in His glory. This is our high calling, and this is our goal: for the Heavens to open so we can experience on Earth the age to come—the longed-for communion between God and humanity.

☞ Reflection Questions ☜

1. What do you think Heaven is like? *intimacy with God A non-stop feeling of connection,*

2. Have you ever experienced worship so natural that you could not stop it? What was that like? *Close and Uninhibited woman of faith freeing*

3. What do you imagine a heavenly atmosphere to be like? *Peaceful and serene, but also exciting*

4. As a child, did you ever experience God's power in a profound way? *No*

5. What do you think the Spirit of Revelation is like?

6. If a door to Heaven opened to you today, how would that experience affect your passion for Jesus Christ? How would it affect your daily life?

7. How would a profound heavenly experience affect a musician? An artist? A politician? A teacher? A businessman? A parent? A minister?

8. Have you ever feared that Heaven won't be worth the earthly price?

9. What is your role on Earth right now? Are you where God has called you to be?

CHAPTER TWO

THE NEW-⊙LD COVENANT

*The LORD God took the man and put him in the
Garden of Eden to work it and take care of it. And the LORD
God commanded the man, "You are free to eat from any tree in
the garden; but you must not eat from the tree of the knowledge
of good and evil, for when you eat of it you will surely die."*

—GENESIS 2:15-17

ADAM AND EVE WALKED IN COMPLETE SPIRITUAL union with their Creator. They didn't need the sun; it stood as a pale reflection to the burning heart of the One who was so full of affection for them.

From the beginning, God's call for humanity has been to a delightful life within an intimate fellowship. His love and pleasure in us was displayed through His creation of the whole universe.

But this union was broken when sin entered the scene. Scripture records in Genesis 3 how God released His judgment in quite an amazing way. First, God cursed Satan for tempting Adam and Eve. Then God promised that out of Eve's womb would come a Deliverer who would destroy the work of Satan forever (Genesis 3:15).

Despite God's judgment on them, Adam and Eve must have been overwhelmed by His compassion! They had failed God, and yet He was already promising them a restoration that would come from their own offspring! The beauty of God's justice was already thawing the icy shame that must have crushed Adam and Eve after rebelling against their Maker.

God gave Adam and Eve an allowance of grace, even though His judgments sustained them outside the realm of divine intimacy, upon which they were dependent. God proved His mercy and goodness right from the start, even from His very first declared judgment, when He cursed their enemies. God also provided a covenant between them, assuring that their lives would be full of purpose.

God rendered judgment upon Eve that she would have pain in childbirth. However, even with this, God spoke forth life—that her womb would be full of children.

God made a covenant relationship with Adam and Eve that reflected His own with us; He told Eve that her desire would be for her husband and that Adam would rule over her.

Eve had completely broken her union with God. Instead of God killing her and making a new plan, though, God told Eve that He wanted to make her life with Adam a picture of the union they had once experienced with God. By this, a divine honor was placed upon Eve in her relationship with Adam, mirroring her divine union with God, which would eventually be restored. I am sure that in God's esteem, Eve carried a nobility unlike any queen we have seen on the Earth.

Adam, too, was spared the punishment of immediate death for his part in the transgression as God further revealed His goodness. God cursed the ground so that it needed to be worked. Before this, the earth had simply produced anything Adam needed. But by this, God created Adam's need to labor. Thus, Adam would experience a function that would bring him satisfaction as well as fulfillment from his work.

God designed the roles of laborer and nurturer, and gave them stewardship over the family, so that together Adam and Eve could enjoy their roles in life. God cared enough about humanity that He created the capacity to enjoy life instead of allowing the misery of sin to rule and reign supreme.

Then, as an ultimate demonstration of His love, God sealed off the Garden of Eden, protecting Adam and Eve from the consequences of eating from the Tree of Life. If they had disobeyed further, and eaten that fruit in their fallen state, their rebellion would have separated them eternally from God.

God released the first couple with the potential for intimacy in their relationship. He also left them with a promise that one day they again might walk in union with Him—seeing their enemies vanquished. This was God's old covenant with humanity.

Solomon's Cry for Wisdom

As we explore God's Word, we find that one of the first people to express frustration with this old covenant and its inherent limitations was wise King Solomon.

One day I had a vision in which I was looking back into history at King Solomon. I could see him in a private chamber. He was in deep thought, poring over the holy books trying to find answers. Solomon was considered the wisest man on Earth, and He was completely stumped for understanding. Days of exploration turned into years of painful unanswered questions.

I saw Solomon trying to discern God's highest truth in a particular matter, which was no little thing. Solomon was expressing the pain of his soul; he entered his throne room, where he had appointed many scribes, and began to shout out his wise frustrations. Men were writing down what he was saying as he proclaimed his struggles with the old covenant. Thus, the book of Ecclesiastes was birthed.

While lodging a complaint about it, Solomon honored the design of the old covenant. He always intimated that our earthly life had a lesser role than what we were created to experience, that we were destined for something eternal. As he expressed in Ecclesiastes, Solomon struggled for a higher mind-set—one that wasn't yet revealed.

But then in my vision, the awesome happened. I saw the years of Solomon's life fast-forwarded, and I saw Solomon when he was much older. He was taken by God to the library room of Heaven and was filled with God's passion for His bride. It was a revelation that few had understood during Israel's history, but Solomon was filled with the desires of Jesus. Solomon began to walk out a prophetic journey of romance on Earth.

Then in the vision, I watched Solomon write the Song of Songs, which speaks of the higher role we are called to play. God was giving Solomon a tasty revelation of divine restoration that offers a promise to us of walking in full communion with our eternal Beloved.

This revelation was higher than what Solomon was living under. I believe it ruined him for God, and his experience restored his life before he died. Through a dim glass, Solomon was able to see Jesus, the Bridegroom.

Although I can't say for sure that all of this happened for Solomon exactly as I saw it, or that he actually wrote Ecclesiastes, I believe my vision offers a true model of how we go through a process of getting filled with God's divine purposes.

The Divine Covenant

When Jesus came to Earth and died for our sins, He provided the "down payment" for humanity's union with God by restoring the original covenant.

Today we partake of the new covenant, which will be complete upon Christ's return to Earth. Jesus' resurrection made the old covenant void. Men and women were no longer under God's judgments for Eve and Adam's sin. God's promise was made complete in the sacrificial death of Jesus Christ. He crushed the head of the enemy and restored the promise to humanity. Jesus did it as the Bridegroom that Solomon envisioned, coming to claim His full reward as a man takes a bride.

God sent John the Baptist to prepare the way for what the Church calls "the new covenant." In a sense, this new covenant is actually more ancient than the old one. It's the covenant of our union with our Creator, which was God's original intent. God never changed His desire or plan for humanity. As the writer of Hebrews states:

> Because God wanted to make the unchanging nature of
> his purpose very clear to the heirs of what was promised,
> he confirmed it with an oath.
>
> —HEBREWS 6:17

John the Baptist was born to help lead God's chosen ones back to their eternal path. Union with God was at hand. The Kingdom was upon them. John allowed his life to be set apart by God—separating himself from experiencing the common human pleasures—so that he could find a deeper life with God.

In his teachings on repentance, John tried to free those who took the old covenant role more seriously than their relationship with God. John was a gatekeeper and a partaker. He taught that restoration was to become the goal of everyone who loves Jesus.

John was able to stand against the religious spirit of the

Pharisees and Sadducees, because he did not recognize the authority of any person who claimed to be God's friend yet was bound by duty rather than by love. John knew that his authority was greater according to an eternal standard, because he did not represent himself. He was sent and commissioned by One who was greater. Therefore, John was not threatened by any human authority not submitted to the Kingdom.

A Higher Love

Since the Fall, humanity has been raised with two primary identities: work and spouse and/or family. These identities are firmly set in the old covenant. What the Pharisees most feared was that John was not proclaiming any value in their roles; in essence, John's message dethroned any real authority to be had in religious identities.

Jesus took it one step further. Building on John's foundation, He said things like: "If you are to be great in the Kingdom, you will be like the least of these."

This is not a statement from a person who cherished status; rather, Jesus taught freedom from all of that. Instead, He established a new goal that would liberate humanity and restore the heavenly possibility of union with God.

As Christians, we should not esteem the same values as the world does—whether we ever chose to be married and have a family or we are considered successful at our labors. As a matter of fact, Paul even encouraged people not to get married, because their time and attention would be consumed with caring for their families.

Paul was not discouraging the idea of marriage; he was refocusing human desires to a higher place. He was conveying that marriage was no longer necessary, since we have the Holy Spirit effectively completing us. Therefore we do not need anything else to complete us—not a job or even a marriage and a family. As believers, we can be fully sustained in God's love by His Spirit.

This idea was unfathomable to a Jewish community dominated

by a religious attitude that substituted God's law for a relationship with God. Some had found such contentment in the law that they worshipped it.

⇐Reflection Questions⇒

1. What has God's Creation shown you about Him?

   His magnificence and majesty and power

2. When you read about God's judgments over Adam and Eve and how merciful God was, do you see any areas in which God may have judged you in the past? Can you see how His mercy ruled in the midst of the judgment?

   1990   Sxc

3. Read Ecclesiastes and the Song of Songs. What are the differences between the two? What are the similarities? What can you learn from both?

4. Have you ever placed your labor for God over your love for Him?

   Tried not too - released from labour right now - to reconnect and deepen my knowledge of Him in Switzerland; and to give me time to socialise, naturally sharing the Gospel as a key part of (my) life.

CHAPTER THREE

THE IDENTITY QUESTION

It is for freedom that Christ has set us free.
Stand firm, then, and do not let yourselves be
burdened again by a yoke of slavery.
—GALATIANS 5:1

THINK ABOUT THE NUMBER ONE QUESTION ADULTS ASK children: "What do you want to be when you grow up?"

Each time I was asked this question as a youngster, my answer changed. One day I wanted to be an astronaut; the next day a movie star. My little friends and I would play games to mimic the roles we coveted in our hearts. By far I was the best rock star among the seven-year-olds in my neighborhood!

Although the question of what we want to become is a practical one, it also can imply that what we do is who we are. In fact, our culture seems to have adapted to this aspect of the old covenant.

Our spiritual freedom in Christ, however, gives us the ability to find our identity in Him—not our job, mate, or family. We no longer need to be defined by our temporal roles. An authority structure is built around our role identities; this structure influences our thoughts, opinions, and behaviors. When we are stripped of the primary need for our temporal identities to define us, it is devastating to anything we have built in the flesh.

The modern Church still supports the old covenant mindset by asking a spiritual version of the question regarding what we want to become. From the time we are new believers, we search for spiritual value in winning souls or in using our gifts and talents to build up the Church.

Hiding Behind Titles

A few years ago at a conference, a member of the host church had experienced a call into ministry. He was definitely gifted. However, as I got to know this man, I realized he was so consumed by his call that his relationship with God was secondary.

Just a few weeks prior to my visit, an itinerant seminar leader told church members: "The Lord wants to reveal your new name, your name that is written on the white stones in the book of life. Just pray, and God will speak this new name to you. He calls some of you 'Apostle,' some of you 'Evangelist,' and some of you 'Servant.' "

During the conference, a young man approached me who was a spiritual son to the pastor. In a deadly serious tone and with the "prophetic stare"—one eyebrow pointing straight up and both eyes penetrating mine—he spoke as if he were about to share with me the mystery of mysteries.

The young man announced: "The Lord has given me a new name! I saw it on my stone. The Lord calls me 'Prophet!' "

My reaction was immediate. I honestly wish I had acted differently, but I did not. I laughed—not in a mean way, but I laughed all the same.

The young man's face contorted, showing his displeasure with my sudden outburst. I knew the situation could easily get out of control if I didn't talk first. So, I instantly responded, not sure if it would get me in more trouble with him than I was already: "I have to be honest with you. The Lord wouldn't call you 'Prophet' as your name. That's like calling you 'My precious refrigerator'. The word prophet is a function, not an intimate name of a friend."

I could see that he was about to defend himself. Clearly I had wounded something deep inside his heart. So I continued to try and explain. "Do you really think the God of Heaven looks at you with such a lack of personal affection? Do you think He would name you after a spiritual role that won't even exist when Jesus comes back?"

"Plus," I continued, "don't you think if God were naming people in this way, it would be sad when you went to Heaven and over a million people would respond when Jesus called out, 'O, Prophet, where are you?' God thinks much more highly of you than that. Consider how He named each person in the Bible with so much care."

However, in an effort to shift his focus toward his relationship with God, I had assaulted this young man's new "identity." So he left angry and hurt. Fortunately his pastor was more mature and later thanked me for my thoughtful rebuke.

Searching for Significance

After people receive salvation, the Church asks: "What has God called you to do?" Or, "What ministry role will you fill in this church?" In a similar way that society says "Your job equals your value," the Church says "Your ministry equals your value to us—and to God." This is the same old covenant mind-set that defined Adam's role as a laborer.

If our value before God is defined by what we do in ministry or for a church, then we land in a very deep pitfall. We begin to believe that we can earn the respect of Heaven by what we do on Earth.

We need to realize that our value comes from deciding to embrace God's love, submitting to the work of the Cross, and its manifestation in our lives. Nothing else.

How do you imagine the apostles have answered the spiritual identity question? Throughout the early Church, leaders functioned via titles that reflected their responsibilities. Their roles were not designed to organize a natural kingdom or to build a self-sufficient community set apart from the rest of the world. Jesus' followers didn't expect to be on the Earth for very long; they were Heaven-bound. Their aim was to prepare people through signs and wonders, teaching, healing, deliverance, and prophecy for Jesus' return.

The apostles helped to promote unity among the believers of Christ, and they focused on sustaining the issue of God's love. Manifesting God's love came first. Church structure was secondary. This is why the Church grew so quickly. People unified in their passion for Jesus, eagerly awaiting His return together.

First-century Christians were regarded as true aliens in this world, rejecting the traditional religious structures of their day—which made them very unpopular. They were filled with awe, praising God daily. Scripture records they were so unconcerned with material success that they shared everything, selling their possessions and goods and giving to those with needs (Acts 2:44). In so doing, Jesus' followers were promoting love more than economic or systematic stability.

⌖Reflection Questions⌖

1. As a child, what did you want to be when you grew up?

2. Have you ever assessed your spiritual value by your performance? *A little with c$$, but with the desire to use my time in a way that roars,*

3. Take some time and bask in God's presence and affection. *pleasing* Ask Him for more of His love. What is He showing you *to God,* about Himself? *I have so much more to, to say teach you in your new Swiss 'home'. thank you for*

4. How would the apostles have defined their spiritual identities?

   — As Jesus' followers

   — Dedicated to Christ

all he has done for me — releasing me into a new life .

CHAPTER FOUR

CALL IT IDOLATRY

One of the teachers of the law came and heard
them debating. Noticing that Jesus had given them
a good answer, he asked him, "Of all the commandments,
which is the most important?" "The most important one,"
answered Jesus, "is this: 'Hear, O Israel, the Lord our
God, the Lord is one. Love the Lord your God with
all your heart and with all your soul and with
all your mind and with all your strength.'
The second is this: 'Love your neighbor as yourself.'
There is no commandment greater than these."
—MARK 12:28-31

SOMETIMES AS I THUMB THROUGH WELL-KNOWN
Christian magazines, I am amused to see all the titles people use
before their names: "Apostle," "Bishop," "Reverend," "Prophet,"
"Worshipper," "Teacher," etc. Although the use of a title is not
wrong in itself, at the same time I wonder if putting such a value
on titles in Christian life could become idolatrous!

When there is pressure to use titles to define spiritual
authority, is it because the title has become part of the community's value system? In the Bible, title defined a function,
not an identity. Likewise, spiritual authority cannot be defined
by a title; it comes from the Lord.

I think this is a very important distinction, because when
people cannot separate themselves from their titles, their
heart and value system seem tied to "position." Again the
mind-set becomes "What we do is who we are." Value is
equated with position.

Realizing this, we can see how the Church reflects society,
rather than influencing it. As followers of Christ, we are called
to bring into the world a higher standard, "pressing on toward
our heavenly goal of Christ."

This fundamental deception regarding titles reaps signifi-
cant consequences in the Church.

The First Consequence
Our identity becomes tied to our obedience to Christ's "second
command" before we fulfill our role within the "first."

In Luke 10, Jesus Himself prioritized two laws:

> Love the LORD your God with all your heart and with
> all your soul and with all your strength.
>
> —DEUTERONOMY 6:5

> Do not seek revenge or bear a grudge against one of
> your people, but love your neighbor as yourself. I am
> the LORD.
>
> —LEVITICUS 19:18

Very few people have a paradigm for ministry that does not view the second commandment (loving others) as the fulfillment of the first commandment (loving God). Few full-time ministries seem valuable to our Church culture unless they spend the majority of their time focusing on getting others closer to God.

But Scripture is clear. Our preoccupation with the first commandment (loving God) produces the second commandment (loving others). When we focus on loving Jesus, the virtue of His love floods us, enabling us to love others with Christ's very love. When we focus primarily on ministering to people, the focus on loving God takes a secondary place in our heart, or sometimes even a lesser place.

Many ministries have codependent relationships with those to whom they minister, because they are completely absorbed in the role of an old covenant laborer. They work to produce a harvest they can see, as opposed to imitating Jesus and living a life of loving God, which bears eternal fruit.

Also, this focus on others can leave us wanting, if our identity becomes tied to helping others. Helping others may then dictate finances, personal happiness, and fulfillment as a man or woman. It is impossible to live under the law and have true fulfillment as a Christian. This misplaced focus is where much of the breakdown happens in relationships, businesses, and ministries.

I have ministered to many leaders who are suffering in ministry, which causes a great suffering in their home life. Their family should help strengthen them during times of strain. Instead, the family falls apart because the relationships have become secondary to the leader, even to his or her ministry. He or she may claim this is not true, but when things begin to break down, it becomes glaringly obvious to everyone. In this way, the Church puts its identity in serving its household even above serving God.

When we study the priesthood in the Bible, we discover that the primary role of a priest is to worship God for His beauty and offer prayers focused on Him. Priests had very real responsibilities to serve people, but they could only do this through their highest role of ministering to the affections of God.

The priesthood was not just a set structure to meet people's needs in relationship with God; priests were called to minister to God's needs on behalf of the people. This is how the identity of leaders in the Church can become healthy again, by becoming a holy priesthood.

The Second Consequence

Because our identity is tied up in the second commandment, ministry, we receive glory for what we do—God doesn't. If my identity is in my ministry, it can become a form of idolatry. I work for it, I produce it, I fulfill it, and I reap from it whether or not the virtue and character of Jesus flows through my life.

Religious work that invests first in people can be done through human power, with or without regard to God. As a result, we as ministers form our identities not in Jesus, but in our ministries. When I cater to other humans who appreciate my work and can express thankfulness, I naturally feel more honored and fulfilled.

But a dilemma emerges when I am fruitless for a season. I will experience the pressures of having done a bad job and wonder if God is unhappy with me. Or if I can build things based on skill, talent, spiritual gifts, and desire, then I may be required to maintain what I build.

One of my spiritual fathers, a prophet named Bob Jones, quips: "If you build it in the flesh, you have to maintain it in the flesh." To me this means we can build many things based on skill, talent, gifting. But if we are not anointed—a product of our union with God—to build these things, and we do it simply based on our desires, then we will have to spend time maintaining them.

A second dilemma emerges as I work within a ministry system. Merely armed with a set of principles, a person can scale a corporate ladder. In a matter of years—with the right politics, the right language, the right look, and the right attitude—an employee can become an essential part of the corporate structure.

The Church often reflects a similar upward mobility. A member who learns the system can, in a brief time, become an influencer. Because the line seems so thin between serving God's will and human will, Christians become more involved with their "image" in a ministry role than with how they please or displease God.

I remember a painful journey when God took me out of what was most valuable to me—the system of ministry. If you build as a community member without, foremost, maintaining a truly loving heart for God, then you will become addicted to the community, which is unhealthy.

So many people become confused by this. A thin line exists between serving God's will and serving the will of people. If you don't make a clear distinction, your value will exist in your role with people, not with God.

When you are involved in the religious system, there can be so much affirmation from people. It is hard not to feel good about what you are doing. But, remember: Where your treasure is, there lies your heart.

God does not summon us to build a good religious structure on Earth. Instead, we are called to wrap up God's inheritance as a gift to Jesus, without having a selfish claim or ownership on those purposes in which we are laboring. Furthermore, the Church is not called to build impressive religious structures here for its own glory.

The Third Consequence
Our devotion and day-to-day relationship with God is either unfocused or hyperactive. A Western mind-set can influence the Church to the point that even our day-to-day devotion to God is tied up in service that is carefully designed by us to gain esteem in the eyes of others.

Drawing our identity from Christ's second commandment to love our neighbors, we lock ourselves into the box of
servanthood, and we miss the freedom of a relationship with
God as His children. This attitude is the number one reason
people in the Church go through periods where their hearts
faint or they become burned-out.

Too many people look for fulfillment in their family, job,
ministry, etc., expecting if they give God their best service, He
will "bless them." Many Christians define this "blessing" as
anything from earthly prosperity to a fulfilled marriage or
even being anointed to minister within religious structures.
This mentality is almost a Christian version of the American
dream: If you work hard enough and find favor with people,
then you will live a fulfilled life with a house, two cars, and
two-point-five kids!

However, such thinking contains both truth and deception.
God does reward our labor, but only if it's in obedience to His
design for our lives. We can do many good acts, but we should
only strive to do the perfected works.

If we don't have a full perspective of God's intentions for
us—to be obedient to His voice for our lives individually—
then this mind-set will cause disappointment with God and
others. It will breed false expectations. "Do good, and you will
be good" is actually an Eastern religious philosophy linked to
karma that has no part in the Gospel.

The Bible is full of stories of God asking for a person's sacrifice, promising a reward in Heaven but not guaranteeing it on
Earth. God asks a high price from us on Earth so that He can
richly reward us in Heaven.

God's first desire for us is to discover a deeply fulfilling
relationship with Him now, which is fulfilled by our divine
union with Him. Everything in the Bible centers around
this concept. God uses suffering in the life He has given
each of us, which further refines our affections for Him. As
the depth of our hearts call out to the depth of His, God
matures our love, stripping us of any other fulfillment.

Thus, we can't help but direct our highest affections to Him. In addition, we receive His highest affections for us—seeing Him in His glory.

God is a jealous Lover. He is so hungry for our identities to evolve from our relationship with Him. Therefore, He will allow our lesser identities to be painfully stripped away from us. He is a desperate Bridegroom, and He wants to receive all that He placed within us.

God actually removes things—sometimes permanently—that we esteem more highly than Himself. As our divine Creator, He knows how to prepare us to "shout from rooftops" that we love Him. We need His help to season our love past a giddy first-love stage for Him. To accomplish this, He sets us on a life course to reposition our passions so they are immersed even more deeply in His love.

If our identities are rooted in our earthly lives, when things go wrong with our church, family, friendships, or jobs, we will feel as if we are failing in these roles or they are failing us. At this point of failure, we will experience deep disappointment and feel a sense of shame in our hearts. Such disillusionment will break our will and cause us to compromise—not just with sin, but even to the point of judging God.

One of the gravest sins is to judge God according to this world's standards, because His word is true and filled with the reality of His goodness. If we doubt this, then we lack confidence in God's nature, and we will not be able to share in His divine virtue. Yet God is pleased with a life that sacrifices everything on the altar of love.

A very close friend, Paula Benne, grew up extremely gifted. She had a great personality, excelled in athletics, and was vivacious in ministering to others. Paula had her whole life planned out, filled with astounding goals. Then one day, God appeared to her in a vision and said: "I want a will exchange. I want you to exchange your highest will for My highest will."

From a human standpoint, Paula's goals were pure and noble, but they were not God-given. In the vision, Paula handed

God all of her hopes, dreams, and aspirations. In return, God gave her a piece of paper that looked like a living will. It contained His plans for her life.

Instead of making her mark by doing extraordinary things in the world, for the past twenty years, Paula has entered into a very private journey involving intercession and delight in God. After all these years, if you asked Paula if she would trade her list with God's, she would reply: "If everything on God's list for my life was going to be fulfilled—no way!" Many Christians find Paula's testimony convicting.

Christianity, unlike any other religion, does not just give acts of service and works a secondary role. God also adopts us as His children and promises us an eternal inheritance, based on our experiences and walk in His love, not based on how much we achieve in the natural.

This means we have the full deed to Heaven that God appointed to Jesus and which He shared with us. The key to these ownership rights is understanding that their nature is not about serving Him but about having an intimate relationship with a loving Father for all eternity.

The Fourth Consequence
We assume that keeping the second commandment results in our greatest reward in Heaven.

When I was a little boy, I remember attending a church service. The preacher greatly enjoyed his own service, but I was bored out of my mind! I thought he was the most monotonous man I had ever heard. But that didn't stop him from assuming we were all experiencing the same rapture he was from his long-winded teaching. During the ministry time, he shouted over the microphone, "This is just what Heaven is going to be like!"

As a six-year-old, my heart just about died. He was saying that Heaven was no better than this church meeting! I looked up at my mother, who was sitting beside me, and declared, "I don't want to go to Heaven!" Shocked, she didn't know what had gotten into me; my statement scared her to death. So she began to pray for me.

This story causes me to smile now, but so many young people do not want to go to Heaven. It's not just their selfish youthful natures wanting to fulfill their dreams before giving everything to God. Rather, it's the attitude that Heaven does not have as much enjoyment as Earth. No wonder so many young people rebel in the Church. Their focus isn't on the eternal hope but on the systems of religion.

This fundamental misunderstanding of Heaven keeps us from desiring it wholeheartedly. The only people who really like Heaven are people who have a hope that it will be nothing like Earth—even church on the Earth.

The Church is called to prepare us for Heaven; it isn't a substitute. Any church that compares itself to Heaven will grieve the Holy Spirit. Let's get real. You wouldn't want to go to Heaven if it resembled one of the church meetings you attend on Earth. We would become so bored after the first few days, let alone the first thousand years!

What we do on Earth does give us a reward in Heaven. Our reward is tied to Jesus, not separate from Him. Some people think of heavenly mansions filled with extravagant items, but even the rich on Earth are not truly fulfilled by material things alone. Wealth by those standards is not an accurate picture of our reward. It's difficult in our fallen state to understand a reward tied to a Person, even if that Person is the glorified Son.

We can capture wonderful glimpses on Earth of our eternal reward that help us rivet our identity to Heaven. Marriage is a dim-glass reflection of how rewarding a relationship can be. But as the days get shorter, marriage is failing to be such a bright picture, even to the Body of Christ. Our heavenly reward is a reward of covenantal relationship that brings total completion. This is what our hope longs for eternally—to be fully united with Jesus.

As I contemplate these questions about eternity, I think of

a quote by Dutch Holocaust survivor Corrie ten Boom, one of my Christian heroes. Toward the close of her life, she made this insightful statement at a public gathering:

> "It was not the ministry that made life worthwhile. It was my journey of watching the faithfulness of God all my days."

⌒Reflection Questions⌒

1. Have you ever sought a title over a relationship?

2. How does influencing society differ from reflecting it? Which do you currently do—influence it or reflect it?

3. What does the term royal priesthood mean to you?

4. What is the current condition of your day-to-day relationship with God?

5. What does loving obedience look like?

6. How have you witnessed the faithfulness of God in your life?

CHAPTER FIVE

Focus On Eternity

You are those who have stood by me
in my trials. And I confer on you a kingdom,
just as my Father conferred one on me,
so that you may eat and drink at my table
in my kingdom and sit on thrones,
judging the twelve tribes of Israel.
—LUKE 22:28-30

WHEN THE DISCIPLES WERE FIRST CHOSEN, THEY HAD no clue what they were getting themselves into. Each one had to be delivered from trying to build a natural kingdom. Until and in some cases even after Jesus' resurrection, the disciples struggled against disappointment in Jesus, because He didn't meet their natural expectations as a leader.

What I find extremely interesting is that Jesus didn't discourage their desire to be influential or powerful. He just refocused their desires onto eternity.

At the same time, Jesus set an incredible example. Instead of setting up an earthly kingdom, He chose to lay it all down. Scripture indicates that people were ready to make Jesus their king by force (John 6:15). But unlike most who are born to rule, Jesus clearly avoided this, withdrawing to a mountain by Himself. The disciples were constantly confused by His restraint. And, in a way, Jesus displayed His most powerful act of love by holding back His glory.

Have you ever wondered what would have happened if Jesus had fully exercised His God-given power? Would every sickness have been healed? Would every grave have been emptied? Would every evil have been rectified? Instead, Jesus moved unhindered among all the earthly needs at hand, focusing His heart and mind on what He must accomplish for eternal purposes.

All the disciples had to reconcile themselves to the truth that Jesus was not living for the establishment of an earthly kingdom. Jesus had already affirmed His followers as eminently important to the Kingdom, but they sought rank and title as well. James and John actually petitioned Jesus to sit at His right hand and left hand. "We are ready to serve You," they said.

But Jesus is worthy of more honor than is contained in the entire Earth. Therefore, He was not preoccupied with establishing an army or a regime. His earthly goal was to obey the Father.

John and James didn't understand all this when they made their request. But Jesus told them, "What you ask is not for me to give, but belongs to my Father in Heaven" (Mark 10:40).

Jesus did not need their service or validation. He was not waiting for His "commanders" to finally understand who He was and then pledge their allegiance to Him. The ultimate picture of this is when the Father picked the day for Jesus to die. His disciples betrayed and abandoned Him. If He had been seeking for them to finally realize who He was, then the Cross was a pretty foolish interruption of that plan.

Jesus was not preoccupied with how His Kingdom was going to be established. He didn't need to establish an army or a regime. His only goal was to obey the Father's voice, recognizing that the Father's will was greater than His own. Jesus knew the Father would give Him much more than anything offered on Earth, because Jesus was born of the Spirit.

Although Jesus did know many things about His journey on Earth, He didn't have foreknowledge of how every step of the Father's will was going to be played out in His life. He was an example of day-to-day communion and obedience. He did not devise a master plan for His destiny based on previously successful works and strategies; He received His destiny by cultivating the Master relationship based on love.

This probably shocked the disciples. They believed Jesus was the Messiah. However, they did not understand that He had not yet claimed His rightful inheritance. Their disappointment was evident.

Paying the Price

In Matthew 20, the mother of James and John requested that Jesus allow her beloved sons to reign with Him for all eternity—permitting one to sit on Jesus' right hand and the other on His left. Their mother was actually fostering a wrong motivation in the hearts of her sons. Don't get me wrong. Her motherly intention was beautiful. I believe that is why Jesus was so gracious with her; He loved her passion for her sons.

Yet Jesus did not give in to her desire. The disciples' families—

and even His own earthly family—were entrenched in wrong understanding! They probably empowered a lot of wrong thinking in one another as they tried to understand this mysterious Christ with whom they spent so much time.

Jesus asked her sons, James and John, if they could pay the price He would pay?

> "You don't know what you are asking," Jesus said to them. "Can you drink the cup I am going to drink?"
> —MATTHEW 20:22

By His question, Jesus refocused their desire on the cost of eternal reward. In this, Jesus went to radical extremes to break their wrong ideals about these earthly processes and natural kingdoms. This was a war that Jesus waged.

Some of Jesus' statements about His own earthly family were considered morally wrong and the ultimate in dishonor by the culture around Him. He explained:

> If anyone comes to me and does not hate his father and mother, his wife and children, his brothers and sisters—yes, even his own life—he cannot be my disciple.
> —LUKE 14:26

Jesus actually said this to the large crowd traveling with Him. The Jewish culture was so wrapped up in the old covenant role of family being one of a person's primary focuses. So, how could they accept such a statement? How could they continue to follow one who did not ascribe value to the central pillar of their culture? Jesus' statement was revolutionary.

This, however, was not the statement of an extremist. It conveyed Jesus' jealous love for humanity. He loved us enough to leave His Father in Heaven, and He expects no less from us—asking us to abandon all other loves for Him. As His followers, we are to treat everything else as lesser in comparison to Him, the greater.

In an epistle, the apostle Paul made an incredible statement about giving up everything that had value to him:

> But whatever was to my profit I now consider loss for the sake of Christ. What is more, I consider everything a loss compared to the surpassing greatness of knowing Christ Jesus my Lord, for whose sake I have lost all things. I consider them rubbish, that I may gain Christ.
> —PHILIPPIANS 3:7-8

Paul considered everything prized by his culture worthless compared with the awesome experience of knowing Jesus. His treasure was in Jesus. Likewise, we need to love Jesus above all else. As He did with the Jewish culture of His day, Jesus calls us to a higher love, to embrace the burning and passionate heart of God.

A People Belonging to God

Speaking about His true family in another situation, Jesus shocked those around Him (as recorded in Mark 3:31-35). The people had announced to Jesus, "Your mother and brothers are outside looking for you." His answer was a question: "Who are my mother and my brothers?" Then Jesus looked at those circled around Him and observed, "Here are my mother and my brothers! Whoever does God's will is my brother and sister and mother."

Jesus confirmed that those who were seeking God's will according to His desire were the only ones He would spend time with—His true brothers and sisters. In this statement, Jesus had separated Himself from the common relationships of the world, and showed His devotion to those who were pursuing eternity. Everything else would represent the world's system, with which Jesus had no part. In this way, He was born of the Spirit, not of the flesh.

Jesus disengaged Himself from the temporal relationships of Earth, demonstrating a new value system. This value system favored relationships that were eternal. In addition, it would not honor relationships that were not eternal.

His rebuke to His mother and brothers was a rejection of the temporary, earthly family unit. It shook up people's thinking about Jesus. How could He claim to be the Son of Love and then reject the ones He was supposed to love the most? He did so by setting a new standard for love!

Jesus cleansed Himself from life's common goals, such as the support of a natural family community that didn't revolve around God's love as much as the love of one another. Jesus was modeling to us how to pursue higher goals.

Later Paul would admonish his spiritual son, Timothy:

> In a large house there are articles not only of gold and silver, but also of wood and clay; some are for noble purposes and some for ignoble. If a man cleanses himself from the latter, he will be an instrument for noble purposes, made holy, useful to the Master and prepared to do any good work.
>
> —2 Timothy 2:20-21

We were never designed to be ignoble, but humanity's fall placed us in this role. Nevertheless, Jesus restored God's desire for us to become a royal people (1 Peter 2:9). We cannot walk in Heaven's nobility unless we cleanse ourselves from all other common identities. Jesus came with words that were sharper than any sword, dividing our understanding about Earth and Heaven, the common and noble, the sacred and the profane.

Unless we enter into our eternal identities, we will not become instruments for noble purposes. We will not enter into a holiness from Heaven. We will not be useful to God. Many people profess faith in God, yet they do not know Him. The reason is obvious—such a relationship costs more than most people are willing to pay.

Paul also spoke about this in Galatians 4, defining the true call of a child of God. He also interpreted one of the Old

Testament stories as a parable for his generation. No longer bound to the things of this world by the old covenant, Paul knew that we could all live as children of true promise. Therefore, we, too, can express the nature of Jesus:

> Now you, brothers, like Isaac, are children of promise. At that time the son born in the ordinary way persecuted the son born by the power of the Spirit. It is the same now. But what does the Scripture say? "Get rid of the slave woman and her son, for the slave woman's son will never share in the inheritance with the free woman's son." Therefore, brothers, we are not children of the slave woman, but of the free woman.
>
> —GALATIANS 4:28-31

It is too easy to be successful by means of our earthly identities. We have the examples and strategies of previous generations to instruct us what not to do. We must travel an incredibly narrow road to be successful in the eyes of Heaven.

The Measure of True Success

A friend of mine had a vision of Heaven. He saw the outer courts, the inner courts, and the Holy of Holies, where Jesus stood. This friend went first to the outer courts, where he encountered many well-known ministers of the last century who had incredible ministries of teaching, healing, and prophecy. Surprised to see them in the outer courts, he approached one of the more famous Christians who had lived during the twentieth century, and asked with genuine interest: "Why aren't you inside with Jesus?"

The man looked at him with a smile. "Because I loved my ministry more than Jesus. I spent more time with ministry to people than I did with Him." The man had no shame and was clearly grateful to be in the company of Heaven. However, my friend was saddened about his own life.

Then my friend was transported into the inner courts,

where he recognized a modern-day hero of the faith. "Why aren't you in the Holy of Holies?" he inquired. This modern-day hero did not take offense at the question but responded truthfully: "I cared more about understanding and wisdom than I did about being with Jesus. My life revolved around an intellectual understanding, not around my relationship with Him." Again my friend was convicted and a little disheartened by what he heard.

Finally he was ushered into the most awesome presence of the Holy of Holies. A radiant love emanated from Jesus. My friend could barely see because of the brilliant light in this room.

Below the throne, he noticed a frail woman holding the hand of God. Searching his memory, my friend could not place her among the leaders of Christendom. Then slowly he walked over to her and discovered that her gaze was fixed on Jesus. Hesitating at first, he finally interrupted her and asked, "Will you tell me who you are?"

Without taking her eyes off Jesus, she replied: "I'm His."

"But how did you get to be in the Holy of Holies?" he asked her.

For a split second, she took her eyes off Jesus to look at him, confused by the question. Her eyes were radiant with the power of His pleasure. She answered: "I just loved Him. All my days on Earth, I only had my love for Him."

"Wow, you must have had an incredible life! What kind of miracles did He do through you?" my friend asked.

She spoke soberly, indicating great brokenness. "Actually, He was the only thing that made my life worth it. I didn't do anything that anyone would consider profound. I just spent my days with Him, because I had nothing else. But He loved me. He is my miracle."

Puzzled, my friend quizzed her further: "Didn't you have a ministry? Some sort of gifting that prepared you for this?"

"No," she replied. "I wasn't very good at anything. I didn't have a good voice to sing to anyone but Him; I didn't have an eloquent speaking ability, so I never taught; I didn't get prophetic words for others. I just loved Him and those He put in my life."

My friend was amazed that someone who seemed to live an unsuccessful ministry life was in the Holy of Holies, so close to Jesus.

This parabolic vision actually depicts how God defines success from Heaven's point of view. It also illustrates how our performance-based attitudes of ministry fall short of what is really important to God.

Jesus is not impressed by our success in anything other than love. As a matter of fact, Jesus demonstrated that He didn't care about our natural success when He spoke in His hometown. Repeating the words of the prophet Isaiah, Jesus told the people:

> The Spirit of the Lord is upon me, because he has anointed me to preach good news to the poor. He has sent me to proclaim freedom for the prisoners and recovery of sight for the blind, to release the oppressed, to proclaim the year of the Lord's favor.
> —ISAIAH 61:1-2; LUKE 4:18-19

Jesus told the people in His hometown that He hadn't come for them but for those who hungered for God. This didn't go over very well with the townspeople; they wanted to kill Him.

Did Jesus feel the sting of rejection in His hometown? No, because He did not come to gain their approval. He came to offer them truth. If they were rejecting this truth, they were rejecting God first, then Him. Jesus was not concerned with His own rejection; He was more concerned with people's rejection of His Father.

In Galatians 5:6, the apostle Paul answers a profound mystery. He tells us the one thing that counts toward our eternal reward:

> The only thing that counts is faith expressing itself through love.

What good is it if we live a successful life in business, ministry, or family but miss the divine invitation to build eternally? The only thing in this world that truly counts is our love for God, expressing itself as obedience to Him through radical steps of faith.

When our emotions are firmly rooted in loving God whole-heartedly, the world's rejection will not carry a sting. We will have the established love of God as our sure foundation.

Reflection Questions

1. Do you desire to be influential?

2. What have you lost for the sake of Christ that you now consider to be profit?

3. What do you say is your most valuable treasure?

4. What does your life actually revolve around?

5. Do your answers to the previous two questions line up with each other?

6. Is the love of God the foundation of your life?

CHAPTER SIX

İnheriting His Reward

Do not store up for yourselves treasures on earth,
where moth and rust destroy, and where thieves break in
and steal. But store up for yourselves treasures in Heaven,
where moth and rust do not destroy, and where thieves
do not break in and steal. For where your treasure is,
there your heart will be also.
—Matthew 6:19-21

ALTHOUGH WE MAY UNDERSTAND GOD'S VALUE SYSTEM, we cannot apply it to our lives until we realize that life is not about us. Furthermore, it is not about us fulfilling a particular role through a ministry on the Earth. If this mind-set describes how we live, our priorities will be out of alignment.

As we understand the larger picture, we will begin to align ourselves properly to an eternal value system. We will long more for our future role in Heaven than for our role on Earth.

First Love

Our first priority is very much related to the first commandment to love God wholeheartedly. God calls us to fulfill the destiny of Jesus, just as Jesus was called to fulfill the destiny of the Father and the Spirit.

Unfortunately the Church has a self-absorbed focus on building its own ministry models and programs and fulfilling the Great Commission according to its own interpretation. Sadly the Church often misses its higher calling. As the Bride of Christ, we are called to minister in a way that helps fulfill Jesus' destiny and purpose.

If I am absorbed in my own individual destiny—and not first by my love for Jesus—then I will be a lover of my own life. Those who truly love Jesus will lose sight of their own goals to walk with Him and become part of His eternal reward.

With a right attitude, the Body of Christ will become capable of great acts of love and unity. We will also be able to experience divine union with God. Wrong priorities, however, violate true love.

Some who have heard God's call to serve run over others in their unswerving drive for success. Jesus, however, opposes this mind-set as arrogance; such thinking is a barrier against spiritual intimacy with Him.

Christians who do not seek unity with fellow believers may discount the effort it requires as being unnecessary. Some may use an excuse of being "on mission" to avoid being unified, seeking to advance their personal accomplishments. Such individuals who achieve their goals by working through human systems will sadly discover that God has nothing to do with it. Many with good intentions may find themselves on the pathway to hell.

At some point, no matter how successful these Christians have been in their labor, they will go through a season where they are completely dissatisfied with their job or their duty—which they often refer to as their "destiny." Some mistake this season as the "dark night of the soul." Contrary to such thinking, though, their season is a gift from God, who seeks to deliver such individuals from their self-centered identities revolving around their desires, not His.

Misguided Endeavors

From the moment we personalize our calling and take on a role of responsibility—with any goal other than loving Jesus—our value will be wrapped up in producing worldly fruit. When this happens, we will become ensnared in the human dynamics that actually hinder our ability to fulfill God's destiny. This is why a political system is so prevalent in our churches. Christians begin to segregate themselves based on doctrine, gifting, or style of expression.

But if our focus is to fulfill the destiny of Jesus, complete unity is possible, even among those who embrace different doctrines, gifts, or styles of expression.

Unity that simply exists for the sake of fulfilling the second commandment, with little concern for the first, will fall short. It is "unity for the sake of unity." Coming together and finding a place of "neutrality" is not enough.

Instead, we need to focus on unity for a higher purpose—Jesus Christ! As we answer His spiritual call, we must never become preoccupied with our role in our personal destiny. Our gaze must remained fixed on Him, understanding that our destiny doesn't just belong in Him—it is Him!

Discovering Your Divine Destiny

In John 17, Jesus prayed that together His followers might

experience the same union He experienced with the Father. This is so profound. If individuals, churches, communities, and entire cities would begin to cry out to their heavenly Father for Jesus to claim His reward, our world would be transformed!

The prophet Malachi had something to say about this:

"They will be mine," says the LORD Almighty, "in the day when I make up my treasured possession. I will spare them, just as in compassion a man spares his son who serves him. And you will again see the distinction between the righteous and the wicked, between those who serve God and those who do not."

—MALACHI 3:17-18

We need to understand God's distinction between doing good and doing evil. God judges us based on the purity of our hearts—not our good intentions.

Are we serving Him, or are we serving ourselves? If we are not serving Him, our hearts are full of impure and carnal motives. Scripture calls us wicked. However, those who turn their hearts fully to God will be counted among His inheritance—His sons and daughters.

The writer of Hebrews takes it one step further, equating spiritual maturity with discernment about what serves Jesus and what does not:

But solid food is for the mature, who by constant use have trained themselves between good and evil.

—HEBREWS 5:14

How do we reach maturity and serve Jesus as He moves toward His destiny? I believe it is by seeing the big goal, not little mile-markers of faith that we often confuse with the finish line.

If we can understand the desperation Jesus feels to inherit His reward, we will never be the same! In fact, Jesus is our reward, and I believe a whole generation will be His inheritance.

Even in the face of death, this generation will see His return. I think the real issue is not so much that we are waiting for Him but that He is anxiously awaiting us!

A Divine Hunger

One day while grocery-shopping, I began to hear a low rumble. Having grown up in California, I had lived through many earthquakes. I expected an earthquake was coming, and so I braced myself for the ground shaking, but nothing happened. Again the sound came, yet no one around me appeared distressed. At that point, I wondered if I was having a spiritual experience! As I got to my car, the sound in my ears grew louder. Finally I asked, "God, what is happening?"

"I am hungry," was His strange reply.

Suddenly I realized those noises were from God's stomach rumblings! He was letting me hear His hunger pangs.

As I began to pray about this, I was led to read Mark 11:12-14:

> The next day as they were leaving Bethany, Jesus was hungry. Seeing in the distance a fig tree in leaf, he went to find out if it had any fruit. When he reached it, he found nothing but leaves, because it was not the season for figs. Then he said to the tree, "May no one ever eat fruit from you again." And his disciples heard him say it.

In this Scripture, Jesus shares a parable that illustrates a divine hunger. Jesus is hungry for the fruit of our lives—the offerings of those whose desire is to feed the heart of God. Jesus longs for the fullness of what was promised to Him by the Father in Heaven.

When you evaluate the hunger of most believers, it is centered around an ambition to see their promises and their desires fulfilled by God. A religious spirit has taught us that God has placed desires in us, and we should serve those desires. People are looking for God to reward them according to their desires, and you know what? He is! I believe this is why there is barrenness in the Church.

But when you look at God's hunger, you understand that we are Jesus' inheritance. We are first and foremost His reward. This is another way to see how people in the Church have a wrong value system. We are His reward before He is ours!

Looking Out for the Interests of Others
Paul tells us about a man who had a unique mind-set:

> I have no one else like him, who takes a genuine inter-est in your welfare. For everyone looks out for his own interests, not those of Jesus Christ.
> —Philippians 2:20-21

It is amazing to me that the apostle Paul found such a mind-set to be rare among believers. It seemed that everyone was looking out for his or her own concerns and importance. Even then, the Church was full of unfruitful fig trees.

Doesn't this sound like the Church today? We try to dis-tinguish ourselves, but those whom Heaven honors are the ones who take a genuine interest in the needs of others who are Jesus' inheritance (Philippians 2:1-4).

Planted to Bring Forth Jesus' Destiny
If Jesus knew it was not the season for the fig tree to bear fruit, as recorded in Mark 11, why would He look at it and curse the little tree? Not only did He create the tree, He created the times and seasons. The answer is found in the analogy of the river of God (Ezekiel 47 and Revelation 22).

God's eternal river flows from the altar below Jesus' throne in Heaven. It streams all the way to Earth. On either side of this river are large trees that are in season every month of the year, yielding twelve crops. These trees are covered with leaves that are full of virtue and that offer healing for the nations.

This river is a metaphor for the destiny of Jesus. As the

river flows into this world, God's Kingdom pours out. Jesus' destiny began to flow as a river from Heaven when He sacrificed everything on the altar of the cross. This river is symbolic of His dominion and inheritance springing forth around the Earth. It is both a literal river of God's presence and also a representation for us of His Kingdom age.

The trees on either side of this river represent people who are planted to bring forth Jesus' destiny. Their roots are nurtured by the water of Jesus' virtues.

Many Christians who have fruit on this level are not seen by those in the world. They remain hidden. Sadly many Christians or organizations serve with the desire to be given their reward in this life, not the one to come. But those who are planted and watered by the river of God experience supernatural fruitfulness and growth. This is what we are called to as sons and daughters of God.

After Jesus cursed the fig tree in Mark 11, Scripture records that He went into the temple in Jerusalem. There He overturned the tables of money changers and halted the flow of money and merchandise through the temple courts. He asked:

> Is it not written: "My house will be called a house of prayer for all nations?" But you have made it "a den of robbers."
>
> —MARK 11:17
> (quoting from Isaiah 56:7 and Jeremiah 7:11)

People had turned the temple into a marketplace, which reflected their human agenda to merchandise the Kingdom of God. Jesus indicated that this was the work of the master thief himself—Satan! Instead, Jesus called Israel back to her primary purpose—to be a house of prayer. He called her to live supernaturally, intimately connected to God's eternal purposes—and not conforming to earthly patterns and lesser purposes.

Jesus continually models how to serve the destiny of One

who is greater. He did not come to serve Himself but to serve His Father. He provides the example of true sacrifice. And then Jesus modeled it as a servant—laying down His rights as a Son.

So why did Jesus curse the fig tree in Mark 11? Why didn't He just command it to bear fruit? I believe He cursed the fig tree because causing it to bear fruit would not resolve the greater problem. This tree was not planted by the river. It did not have the capacity to be always in season. It was not of Him.

Just as the fig tree was cursed, so the temple was a cursed, fruitless institution. Jesus actually cursed the temple practices; out of mercy He also re-focused them as well. As always, when Jesus judges, it is with the hope of calling us higher.

Unfortunately, much of what happens in the name of God today is like that barren fig tree. It may appear to be full of green leaves—looking full of life and healthiness—but it is not full of fruit. As a result, Jesus has no choice but to curse what does not bear the fruit He hungers for.

In the coming years, we will see a landslide of failing religious activity in both well-known and unknown churches. Their activity will flicker and fade away, because it does not serve Christ's destiny.

As the disciples were walking down the road, they observed the fig tree that Jesus had cursed. Peter noticed the tree had simply shriveled up and died. Recognizing the disciples' amazement, Jesus challenged them:

> "Have faith in God," Jesus answered. "I tell you the truth, if anyone says to this mountain, 'Go, throw yourself into the sea,' and does not doubt in his heart but believes that what he says will happen, it will be done for him. Therefore I tell you, whatever you ask for in prayer, believe that you have received it, and it will be yours."
> —MARK 11:22-24

Jesus was speaking about the fruit that results from the authority of those who serve Him. They would do unimaginable things. But the fruit would evidence a life of prayer and a faith focused solely on God.

In addition, if we understand that the fig tree represents religious structures not planted by the river, then we see that life planted in Jesus' destiny will produce astounding fruit.

For example, if you are praying for something that lines up with the calling of Jesus, it will be done. If you pray against something that is trying to stand in God's way and you believe that Jesus is worthy to inherit all of His reward, then what you pray will also be done. Whatever we ask for with this kind of passion for Jesus cannot be denied to us, or Him! If asked in faith, it will be given completely, because it is for His sake.

⟜ Reflection Questions ⟞

1. What are your priorities in life and ministry?

2. What does unity in Christ look like to you?

3. What is the goal God has set for us?

4. What is God hungry for? What nourishment can you give Him?

5. Are there agendas in your life that need to be laid down for the sake of Christ?

CHAPTER SEVEN

YOUR SAVIOR COMES

The voice of one crying in the wilderness:
"Prepare the way of the LORD;
Make straight in the desert
A highway for our God;
Every valley shall be exalted,
And every mountain and hill brought low;
The crooked places shall be made straight
And the rough places smooth;
The glory of the LORD shall be revealed,
And all flesh shall see it together;
For the mouth of the LORD has spoken.
—ISAIAH 40:3-5a

THE PROPHET ISAIAH FORETOLD OF A COMING GLORY to be revealed to humanity. Thus we are the gatekeepers of God's promise. Our role is to prepare the way for the Lord Jesus to receive His eternal reward. If we understand our role, we can walk in full spiritual authority on the Earth, despite any opposing power.

The prophet Elijah was empowered to face evil, despite the fact that other prophets backed off in fear for their lives. On behalf of his beloved Lord, Elijah stood alone to face one of the world's worst manifestations of the spirit of Jezebel. Instead of being overcome by his human weakness, Elijah trusted in the living God!

Focused on God

Hundreds of years later, John the Baptist carried the spirit of Elijah, following in Elijah's footsteps. Despite the religious spirit operating in his generation, John cried out for repentance. Even though he was one of the most charismatic voices of his time, John knew his role in eternity.

John didn't get sidetracked by fame. Rather, he exercised his ability to lay down everything. This attitude distinguished him from others. John was so focused on serving Jesus that he lived unselfishly. He did not try to become a successful voice among the people, even though he had one of the most powerful, charismatic speaking abilities given to a human. He remained focused on God.

Later Jesus said of John the Baptist: "He was the most powerful prophet to ever live." John didn't vie to outperform other prophets through his prophetic utterances. There is no record of miracles or healings that he performed. Yet John's ability to lay down everything and make a way for Jesus to enter into His destiny distinguished his life for eternity.

In Heaven, I believe that John has a primary role in serving God, because he laid no claim to own an earthly ministry calling. John gained nothing on Earth. Rather, he humbly laid down his life as an offering, with the prayer that Jesus would receive His complete reward.

A Forerunner Spirit

We can perceive and grab hold of a radical passion modeled by John's life. John was a forerunner heralding a new age. Therefore, when we see people who are sick, and who are a part of Jesus' reward, we need not ask ourselves whether we have the gift of healing before we try to heal them. In faith we can pray for them to be delivered, because they belong to Him!

We need not wonder whether we have the gift of prophecy in order to proclaim God's heart upon the Earth. We need to boldly make prophetic declarations that release God's full inheritance to Jesus, without waiting for others to do it. If we are consumed with the desire to furnish Jesus with His inheritance, then we will become the vessels of honor that deliver it to Him.

As we grasp this understanding, we will no longer look for our place in the Body of Christ, or ask what kind of gifting we have. We will do whatever we can to give Jesus what belongs to Him, at any cost.

I have seen a quiet, small woman roar the word of the Lord powerfully when gripped by this reality. Passion is not determined by a person's nature or personality type; it's a measure of the degree God's divine nature has been imparted to us, so that we can call upon His name and accomplish His desire.

When we begin to abandon our understanding of who we are to gain a greater understanding of who He is, then our lives cry out to Him: "You are worthy!" Then, and only then is Jesus able to receive His due. For this to occur, like John the Baptist, we must decrease so that God might increase.

When many begin to walk with this forerunner spirit, or with a John-the-Baptist heart, the promise in Joel 2 will begin to be released upon the world. A token of this promise was experienced by the disciples gathered in the upper room on the day of Pentecost (Acts 2). Their lives were changed forever.

God's Bondservants

In the last days, the Earth will witness an unprecedented movement of God's Spirit that will be released through the lives of Christians who have turned their hearts fully to knowing and being known by Jesus. They will be His bond-servants. God will be able to move through these people for one reason alone: Their hearts will so totally belong to eternity that God's Spirit will flow powerfully through them, allowing them to do signs and wonders and perform healings that will be astounding.

These bondservants will have a love for God that mirrors God's love for them:

> For God so loved the world that he gave his one and only Son, that whoever believes in him shall not perish but have eternal life. For God did not send his Son into the world to condemn the world, but to save the world through him.
>
> —JOHN 3:16-17

God's goal in this end-time outpouring of His Spirit is for the entire world to be redeemed. This is what God promised Jesus if He would pay the price for it. God will not fall short of giving Jesus everything that belongs to Him. Therefore, He will empower us with the Spirit, which he gave Elijah and John the Baptist, if we will only appropriate the fullness of living for Him.

Do you realize that God wants to save an entire genera-tion as His Son's reward? It's not just the accumulation of many generations. God wants an entire generation of the world to cry out to Him with the longing to have His glory pass before us, so that we would fellowship with Him in the way He desires!

What would happen if the Body of Christ in this age began to cry out together, making their worship a house of prayer for the desire of God to be fulfilled? I believe that billions of peo-ple would be saved in a single generation! Then Jesus would step off His heavenly throne and rush to Earth as described by the prophet Isaiah:

The LORD has made proclamation
　to the ends of the earth:
"Say to the Daughter of Zion,
　'See, your Savior comes!
　　See, his reward is with him,
　and his recompense accompanies him.' "
　　　　　　　　　　　　　　—ISAIAH 62:11

⌔Reflection Questions⌔

1. What inspires you about the life of Elijah?

2. What inspires you about the life of John the Baptist?

3. What inspires you about the life of Jesus?

4. Who is Jesus to you? Is that intimacy with Him growing?

5. What would happen if the Body of Christ began to cry out together for God's desire to be fulfilled? How can you help that process?

CHAPTER EIGHT

A God-Inspired Heart

One thing I ask of the LORD,
this is what I seek:
that I may dwell in the house of the LORD
all the days of my life,
to gaze upon the beauty of the Lord
and to seek him in his temple.
—PSALM 27:4

GOD IS LOOKING FOR A QUALIFIED HEART FOR ETERNITY. Humanity as well as our demonic foe will confuse us by suggesting a million things we must do to become qualified—to be really used by God or to be worthy of His love. But God Himself is looking for just one thing—our passionate desire for Him.

In Scripture we find a desperate father who petitions Jesus on behalf of his only son (Luke 9:38-40). The son is demonized, and evil spirits regularly threaten his survival. When the disciples had failed to deliver his son from evil, the man's faith was probably shaken.

So he implores Jesus: "If you can help do anything, have compassion and help us" (Mark 9:22b).

Picking up on the doubting words of the father, Jesus responded with a merciful rebuke: "If I can?" repeated Jesus (Mark 9:23). "Everything is possible for him who believes!"

The deciding issue was not Jesus' power but the man's faith. Jesus' reply must have powerfully provoked this father's heart. He cried out tearfully, "Lord, I believe; help my unbelief!" (Mark 9:24). The father asks Jesus to remove all doubt and grant him unwavering faith. And the son was healed.

Radical Leaps of Faith

Likewise, as we make radical leaps of faith, our most appealing cry to God's ears may be the "yes!" that breaks through our unbelief: "God, I do believe, even though I am not yet entirely convinced. Please help me overcome my stronghold of doubt!"

The preceding story is one of the great parables illustrating the "yes" God desires to hear from us. Despite our unbelief, God is inspired when we make a radical leap of faith, crying out, "Yes, God, I believe, although not all of me is convinced!"

God knows that we have a "no" in our heart; He is fully aware of our doubt and unbelief. Even so, we inspire His intervention when we adopt the humble cry of desperation: "Lord, I do believe; help my unbelief!"

God is not expecting us to be perfect in our nature. He only requires us to have the humility to acknowledge that we are weak outside of Him and that we cannot overcome our strongholds without His help. This attitude is what qualifies us before God's throne—a "yes" that is larger than our "no." It is not always a "yes" instead of a "no," but it is when the "yes" of our heart dominates our very being despite our "no." This kind of love inspires the heart of God.

Satan and humanity will suggest or imply that we need to do a million things in order to qualify for God's love. Playing on our doubt and unbelief that God could truly love us with an everlasting love, Satan blinds us with condemnation and shame. He counterfeits God's inspiration and substitutes immediate gratification. He conspires with our wicked desires.

Even as the "yes" to God's invitation pounds in our heart, our fallen nature somehow resists this great desire for God.

Temptations and Dilemmas

Why does God allow such temptation to bombard our minds and distract us? Perhaps it is so we can build up a strong resistance to carnality. Or so He can clearly demonstrate how His strength counteracts our weakness. Or perhaps God realizes that after we fall, we will experience His strength and thus, cry out for His help again.

King David's life demonstrates how, despite great brokenness and poor choices, we can always return to God. David cultivated a deep love for God, mixed with humility, which is beautifully reflected in this psalm:

> One thing I ask of the LORD,
> this is what I seek:
> that I may dwell in the house of the LORD
> all the days of my life,
> to gaze upon the beauty of the Lord
> and to seek him in his temple.
>
> —PSALM 27:4

David's one desire was to be in union with the Lord throughout his life; he longed to gaze upon God's beauty and to be completely fulfilled by what he saw. David's passion inspired the heart of God, causing Him to move on David's behalf. Why? Because David was not focused on his lesser desires and an earthly destiny. His sole longing was for God.

Many of us face a divine dilemma, which the enemy constantly tries to use to his advantage: We have a "yes" in our heart, but there always seems to be a part of our fallen nature that resists the great desire for God.

Satan magnifies our unbelief within our hearts. He wants to inspire wicked desires within us that agree with our carnal "no." He continually tries to counterfeit God's inspiration by offering immediate gratification on earth, in place of what God is offering in Heaven.

Thankfully because of the grace God extends to us, Satan is not powerful enough to disqualify us. Nevertheless, he knows we can disqualify ourselves. So his mission is to strengthen our unbelief by presenting opportunities that tempt us to give ourselves over to our wicked desires.

One of the principles confusing many believers is that God allows us to experience this process of temptation and distraction. He does this so that we can build up resistance to our carnal nature, which asks us to choose ourselves instead of Him. God allows this failure, knowing that He is the answer to our very weakness. Therefore if we taste God's strength and then fall in our weakness, we will cry out for His strength again. David did this so many times, appealing to the merciful nature of God.

The Choice to Love

Jesus makes the choice clear, but He gives us the freedom to make it. The enemy tries to use our failures to reinforce our shame, but God uses our failures to draw us to Himself.

David inspired God's heart, because he knew the only thing that qualified him before God was his willing heart. How could a man like David, who had lied, fornicated, cheated, and murdered, be considered a man after God's own heart? It was his heart, not his performance. Despite his brokenness, David constantly came back to the "yes" that was in his heart. He overcame in much the same way that God invited the churches of Revelation to overcome.

How can we transform our bent toward worldliness? For many years, Mike Bickle has been a voice crying in the wilderness, offering hope to those bound in shame. He has expressed this hope in his messages drawn from a passage in the Song of Songs 1:5, "I am dark, but I am lovely!"

The cry of the Shulamite woman, who was a laborer in the fields, came from a desperate soul who saw nothing in herself that would draw the esteem of King Solomon. Yet he loved her. When she experienced the intensity of his love, she concluded, "Even though my skin is darkened, and I may appear worthless to others, Solomon loves me! He looks at me and sees a woman who is beautiful and worthy of his affection!"

The Shulamite woman had a revelation of what it truly means to be loved. She was empowered by Solomon's love for her, embracing the loveliness he saw in her. Thus she could grow secure in his love.

Even as a "yes" resonates in our hearts, we may be conveying to God: "I am not worthy. I am not like you. My heart is dark and shameful." Yet God's burning desire to commune with us captures our hearts so intensely that we can say, "Even though I am dark, I am lovely in your eyes!"

God's love is our qualifier.

⌐ Reflection Questions ⌐

1. Is there any unbelief in your heart that needs to be broken?

2. Why does God allow us to be tempted?

3. What inspires you about the life of David?

CHAPTER NINE

THE LONGING FULFILLED

Hope deferred makes the heart sick,
but a longing fulfilled is a tree of life.
—PROVERBS 13:12

AFTER HIS RESURRECTION, JESUS APPEARED TO THE disciples (Luke 24). Distraught by His absence, they were finally in a place where He could give them understanding, since they were so full of joy because everything He had said to them had proven true! They were caught off-guard by all the Old Testament prophecies their beloved Friend had fulfilled

Their passion for Him fed His hunger! I am going to infer even a greater meaning in His hunger. Jesus was not hungry for nourishment. He was actually communicating to the disciples that they could now feed His hunger. They had passed from desperation into true love for Him. Jesus took the food they offered and ate it.

Previously the disciples had been unable to comprehend the Scriptures about His crucifixion and resurrection. Then Jesus opened up their minds to understand the Scriptures regarding Himself. Jesus was then able to interpret those teachings in light of His destiny and how the Scriptures were fulfilled.

Feeding God's Hunger

Jesus longs to share who He is with us in a mature way so that we can partner with Him as a wife to a husband. Do you want to feed God's hunger with your passion?

When His love is first awakened in us, Jesus draws us through various stages. The first stage is one of "first love," introducing us to God's awesomeness. The second stage is one of "fiery love," expressing a strength that makes us feel as though we can conquer the world. The third stage is one of "covenant love," involving His sweet communion. And the fourth stage is one of "desperate love," where we are longing for His presence.

Most Christians miss the opportunity to enter into the fullness of God's love, although He stokes this desperate love within us on more than one occasion. At times, we may even fear that we have disqualified ourselves from such love!

It is hard for most people to allow themselves to experience the exquisite pain that comes with the depths of desperate love.

Jesus allows our pain to exceed the level we imagined we could handle. He strips away every unnecessary thing—and person—that might provide us comfort. We become absolutely lonely to experience Jesus. Then He begins to stir up within our heart the desire to be one with Him—just as He is one with the Father.

Distracted by a Lesser Love

If a person's identity is wrapped up in worldly pursuits (even noble ones), it will be easy to give in to a lesser love than God. Compromise occurs when we substitute God's offer with a less satisfying earthly role, lifestyle, or relationship.

How this longing for God is fulfilled can be illustrated by looking at young people. When love awakens in them, often a desperation ensues. Instead of pressing with hearts, minds, and souls toward God, teenagers in church begin to look for a human "counterpart." Turning their eyes from God, they seek a mate.

Often when God is ready to awaken a full and intense love for Himself, the Church culture suggests marriage as the highest calling. This, though, is a counterfeit for a higher, more fulfilling love. If, during this season, young people begin to substitute a person for God, it can be spiritually costly. If they have not resolved their identity issues before God, this love is twice as difficult to express later, when their lives are filled with responsibility toward a mate and family.

Christianity is unique in its focus on humanity's relationship with God. Teachers of Islam often encourage young men to be martyred, believing they will garner a harem of virgins for eternity. Mormons believe that each adherent and spouse will inherit a whole world to populate. The New Age offers humanity the opportunity to merge into a universal consciousness or energy as their eternal reward.

From the days that God walked with Adam and Eve in the Garden of Eden, God has desired that humanity find delight in communion with Him. So I wonder why we encourage Christians to form lasting human ties so quickly?

Fueled by a Desperate Love

Modern Church thinkers may look on early Christian writers—some considered saints by the Catholic Church—as eccentric or mystical. Their poetic language conveys a longing for God that most people with an analytical mind-set do not understand. However, it would be helpful to examine the lives of these saints, who wholly engaged themselves in their pursuit in God, and often paid a high price—martyrdom—for their faith. Dying as martyrs was their final expression of true love.

St. John of the Cross was one such Church father known for a passionate pursuit of God. He was so devoted to God that he declared, "Your love has wounded me!"

To move forward in our relationship with God, I believe we have to experience such passion. We will never fully unite with Jesus unless we face the same disillusionment process as the disciples—one of longing and disappointment in this world.

Sometimes experiencing this kind of passion can be all-consuming and overwhelming. Much of the Western Church discourages people from being sensitive to these realities, because they are afraid of the imbalance such awareness creates.

I believe we have to experience such emotions, even if they may seem extreme. In this way, we can find our balance by His affections. If believers who profess love for God have never been through this inward longing, their love probably has not progressed very much. Such a statement will threaten those religious leaders who understand the politics of worldly systems but who do not know how to experience the depths of Christ.

Modern Christianity often misleads its own disciples, suggesting that once we give ourselves to Jesus, we will never again long for anything. Life will be complete, with no more heartache. However, this is not true.

Our passion and desperation for God occurs not once, but repeatedly and cyclically, as God continually turns our gaze toward eternity. The more our affections belong to God, the less satisfied we are with Earth; we begin to feel as Paul describes:

> Meanwhile we groan, longing to be clothed with our
> heavenly dwelling, because when we are clothed, we will
> not be found naked. For while we are in this tent, we
> groan and are burdened, because we do not wish to be
> unclothed but to be clothed with our heavenly dwelling,
> so that what is mortal may be swallowed up by life.
>
> —2 CORINTHIANS 5:2-4

Paul is not describing an intellectual appeal. Rather, such
longing is designed to lead our hearts in pursuit of eternity.
This wasn't just a clever idea; it was Paul's life-pursuit.
Regardless of difficulties and hardships, Paul would not compromise the very thing he desired most—being in Heaven.

The more we open ourselves to the kind of longing and
desperation Paul had for the eternal, the more understanding
Jesus will give us. While we will never understand the mind of
God, we will find His blessings when we believe and pursue
what we cannot even imagine seeing!

In Lovesick Pursuit

We are never qualified by a ministry position or a particular
spiritual gift. Instead we are qualified by our pursuit of God's
loving fellowship. The beloved apostle John tried to express
this when he wrote:

> This is how we know that we love the children of God:
> by loving God and carrying out his commands. This is
> love for God: to obey his commands. And his com-
> mands are not burdensome, for everyone born of God
> overcomes the world. This is the victory that has over-
> come the world, even our faith.
>
> —1 JOHN 5:2-4

John said we love one another by first loving God and then
carrying out His commandments. Not the other way around. In
fact, it is impossible truly to love others first and then carry out

God's commands. It would be like trying to sail without a ship. The ship must come first; then you have something to sail.

John was fully devoted to sacrificing everything in order to please God, who was his best Friend. Fulfillment of the second commandment—loving others—comes from an overflow of our devotion to God. As we do this, our hearts become opened to a supernatural virtue: to love in a way that is uncommon on Earth.

"I have food that you know not of," said Jesus to His friends when they became worried that He was not eating with them. As we learn to feed on His presence, we discover a love that will truly unite hearts, feeding the soul's frenzy within. In this way, we can begin to say "I have food that you know not of" just as Jesus told His friends when they expressed concern that He was not eating with them.

When our primary sustenance is communion with God, we will finally say, "I cannot be satisfied with anything earthly. My desire reaches beyond this world into communion with God— and into obedience to His plan for the Son."

If our longing is for Him, then we will be fulfilled. In communion, we will all eat from the Tree of Life. But if we hope in promises for ministry or for gain, the perfect mate or the perfect church, then our hopes will be deferred. These things are lesser hopes.

As it is written in Proverbs 13:12: "Hope deferred makes the heart sick, but a longing fulfilled is a tree of life."

⌒ Reflection Questions ⌒

1. When was the last time God was nourished by your fellowship?

2. What awes you about the love of God?

3. Have you ever experienced a desperate love for God?

4. How deep is your longing for God?

5. What does this phrase by St. John of the Cross mean to you: "Your love has wounded me!" How does love inflict a wound?

6. How would you describe your pursuit of God's fellowship?

CHAPTER TEN

To Kn⊙w the Unkn⊙wn

Paul then stood up in the meeting of the Areopagus
and said: "Men of Athens! I see that in every way
you are very religious. For as I walked around
and looked carefully at your objects of worship,
I even found an altar with this inscription:
TO AN UNKNOWN GOD. Now what you worship
as something unknown I am going to proclaim to you."
—ACTS 17:22-23

ONE NIGHT AS I WAS LEAVING MY HOUSE TO ATTEND A service at the House of Prayer in Kansas City, God spoke to me: "Bring your cell phone. I am going to call you."

At first I was nervous because His voice was so clear, and I did not understand how the Lord would call me on my cell phone! Intrigued and eager to see the miraculous, I responded to the Lord:

> "I don't want to disrespect Your desire, but I am going to leave my cell phone here. If You want to call me, there are pay phones where I am going. Or my friends have cell phones. Or You could even bring my cell phone to me supernaturally."

As odd as this may seem, I believe that God divinely motivated me toward this resolve. I challenged God, because I was truly excited about His word. I didn't test Him; instead, in faith, I made the fulfillment of this word even harder to accomplish in the natural.

Then I left for the meeting. It was a cold night, and I was wearing my jacket. Toward the end of the meeting, I began to walk outside, when a good friend stopped me to talk. We chatted for a few minutes. I stuffed my hands into my jacket pockets while we talked. After taking my right hand out of my jacket pocket to scratch my chest, I placed it back inside the pocket. Suddenly, my face turned white—my cell phone had miraculously materialized in my jacket pocket.

Seeing my astonishment, my friend asked if everything was okay. Pulling out my cell phone, I stared at it intensely. Then I related my conversation with God to my friend, and we both stared at the phone.

We were standing inside a building in which I had never been able to receive cell-phone reception. Suddenly the phone showed that it was searching for service. It rang, just as I finished telling my friend why I was so surprised to find my cell phone. We both looked down at the phone. The caller ID read "unknown." Although I had received thousands of calls on this phone in the last five years, "unknown" had never appeared before on my cell phone. Stunned, I let my phone ring until my friend finally said, "Answer it!"

Sheepishly I clicked on talk and hesitantly said, "Hello?" No one answered. I waited awhile and just kept saying "Hello?" but when I looked down it was searching for service again.

I excused myself from my friend and hurried outside. I got on the phone and called my friend Paul Keith Davis. After recounting what had happened, I asked him, "What do you think this means?" He intuitively replied, "This is about the unknown God that Paul talked about in Acts."

Just as he said this, the phone beeped, even though I was still talking with him on my cell phone. My call waiting was activating. Take a guess what the caller ID read—"unknown"! I freaked out, telling Paul Keith to hold on: "I think God is calling me again." I clicked over to answer the other phone line.

"Hello?"

There was no answer.

"Hello?"

Still nothing.

"God, is this You?" I asked.

The line clicked off, and I went back to the line where Paul Keith was holding. "It was the unknown again!" I said, puzzled.

Later I called my phone company to have them track the calls, in case it was a sales call. They said there was no record of either call! The phone company could see that I had received some incoming calls earlier that day, but those two particular calls did not register in their database. These calls didn't appear on my telephone statement either, although every call shows up.

In the Scripture passage referencing the unknown God (Acts 17:22-23), the apostle Paul was addressing the Greeks in Athens, who had idols for almost every god. Not wanting to offend a god they had never heard of, the Greeks built an altar dedicated "to an unknown God."

The apostle Paul looked at this altar and declared to them: "What you worship as something unknown I am going to proclaim to you" (Acts 17:23b). Then he revealed this unknown God to them further and explained:

> God did this so that men would seek him and perhaps reach out for him and find him, though he is not far from each one of us. "For in him we live and move and have our being." As some of your own poets have said, "We are his offspring."
>
> —Acts 17:27-28

Our Deepest Longings

As he unveiled this unknown God to the Greeks, Paul shed light on a deeper understanding about the "meat" for which we all truly long. I believe God's greatest desire when He created humanity was to share with us the most precious quality about Himself—His identity.

It would be enough if God simply loved us, and let us serve Him. Instead, He longs to share His divine nature with us, not just in the outer courts, but in His innermost sanctuary—His throne room. He wants to impart to us the fullness of who He is. God does not want to remain unknown to us.

The enemy's strategy of tempting us to wear our own identities is a lesser role than what God desires for us; it also hinders us from truly sharing in God's identity.

No other world religion has the focal point of a deity who shares himself with his followers, in covenant relationship, and in love. All other gods written about have a selfish focus; they reward people only for acts of service to the deity's own agenda. Jesus is the only sacrificial God. He longs to share Himself with those who would love Him, offering them His free gift of love. This is what sets Christianity apart from other religions. In addition, it makes it impossible to accomplish anything without His supernatural help.

God wants to be known. He longs to call each one of us and personally share His nature with us—not just in His outer courts but with us standing in His very Presence.

Our Desire to Be Known

This desire for divine intimacy is expressed by Jesus when He announces that God's Spirit will dwell within us.

> I will ask the Father, and he will give you another Counselor to be with you forever—the Spirit of truth. The world cannot accept him, because it neither sees him nor knows him. But you know him, for he lives with you and will be in you.
>
> —John 14:16-17

God's dwelling place inside us addresses our greatest need—to be fully known and understood. God is the answer to the deepest longing of our hearts.

When people share that their struggles relating to God feel one-sided, I don't doubt their frustration. I have experienced many seasons like this. But I discovered the problem was not with God. It was with me. I wasn't fully engaged in relating with God. As I passionately pursued Him, I found a wonderful surprise of His intimate presence.

God Reveals His Identity

In Exodus 33, we read that Moses longed for deeper fellowship with God. Moses was the first one in Scripture who expressed this greater desire. He was not content simply to be known by God; Moses wanted to know God's identity—His divine essence.

> Moses said to the LORD, "You have been telling me, 'Lead these people,' but you have not let me know whom you will send with me. You have said, 'I know you by name and you have found favor with me.' If you are pleased with me, teach me your ways so I may know you and continue to find favor with you. Remember that this nation is your people."
>
> —Exodus 33:12-13

Can you imagine how pleased God was with Moses' desperate cry? Moses wanted to know God intimately. No wonder Moses was the first human that God called "friend." Although Enoch walked with God, and Abraham was called God's friend, no previous biblical recording indicates that anyone ever expressed the desire for such close fellowship with God. Consequently, a further encounter took place between Moses and God:

> And the LORD said to Moses, "I will do the very thing you have asked, because I am pleased with you and I know you by name." Then Moses said, "Now show me your glory." And the LORD said, "I will cause all my goodness to pass in front of you, and I will proclaim my name, the LORD, in your presence. I will have mercy on whom I will have mercy, and I will have compassion on whom I will have compassion. But," he said, "you cannot see my face, for no one may see me and live." Then the LORD said, "There is a place near me where you may stand on a rock. When my glory passes by, I will put you in a cleft in the rock and cover you with my hand until I have passed by. Then I will remove my hand and you will see my back; but my face must not be seen."
>
> —Exodus 33:17-23

Certainly Moses was overjoyed. He may have wondered why he could not look upon God's face, the most distinguishing of features. However, Moses could clearly hear God's voice:

> Then the LORD came down in the cloud and stood there with him and proclaimed his name, the LORD. And he passed in front of Moses, proclaiming, "The LORD, the LORD, the compassionate and gracious God, slow to anger, abounding in love and faithfulness, maintaining love to thousands, and forgiving

wickedness, rebellion and sin. Yet he does not leave the guilty unpunished; he punishes the children and their children for the sin of the fathers to the third and fourth generation."

—Exodus 34:5-7

As God passed by, proclaiming His name and character to Moses, I wonder if angelic gasps echoed through the halls of Heaven! God was sharing with Moses what had been previously unshared, except with Adam. God was sharing His identity—the attributes that make up who He is—with a human. God related to Moses on terms that He knew would give the greatest understanding this side of eternity.

God declared, "I AM that I AM." Who is this God who shares His holiness with His creation? Who is the One who continues to grant the power of His name to people today?

Jesus as the Expression of God

When God's Son came to Earth, God gave Him the name Jesus. Angels and demons alike must have been in such awe when the name was first spoken forth by the angel Gabriel to Mary. God's identity was finally being revealed to humanity! That was one of the most exciting days in history, and I cannot wait to watch the replay when I get to Heaven!

As Jesus' name was spoken, it contained incredible power. It wasn't just an identifying title, but His name holds the full virtue of who He is. Even those who didn't know Him can invoke the authority of His name; they can exercise power over demons by using the name of Jesus! Once He revealed the name, His unchanging nature was embedded in it.

What kind of God shares His identity with a fallen people, who so easily misuse it? A God whose heart is ravished by the very humanity He created.

Isn't it just like Satan to try and keep Jesus' name as the most cursed word among modern languages? Hollywood uses the name Jesus as a curse word more than any other foul words put together. The Spanish, Italian, English, and many other cultures use His name as a profanity.

Satan, of course, is going to make every effort to familiarize us with the name Jesus, not as our Savior God, but as a curse. Our foe wants to bring an over-familiarity with the name to dilute the purity of its divine virtue. However, the devil will pay a big price for doing this; no matter how the name of Jesus is said, it is His name, and therefore, it holds His virtue.

Jesus' Virtue Prevails

This reminds me of the amazing testimony of a friend. Before he became a follower of Jesus, he was bitter and complained often. Troubled by a chronic back injury, he leaned over one day to pick up something. Sharp pain shot through his body, and he let out a curse. "Jesus Christ!" he said, grabbing his back. At that moment, he felt the presence of God—and his back was completely and instantly healed.

Stunned, he told God: "If You love me enough to heal my back when I call Your name as a cuss word, then You can heal all of me." As he trembled with fear, the saving power of Jesus flooded into his life.

The name of Jesus is a passionate doorway into His heart and virtue. Once a friend and I went to the movies to watch a film many from the Christian community were hailing as an allegory that spoke powerfully to the Church. But actually the film was full of compromise. At one point, the main character cursed, saying "Jesus!" During the movie, I noticed a cloud descend over the audience. It was not smoke, but it was opaque. In the midst of it, I could feel God's presence. The Holy Spirit said to me: "Even a curse cannot hold back My virtue!"

God's holy name never changes. It is always full of power and glory. We enter into intimate communion with Him as we begin to meditate and contemplate the virtue and identity contained in God's name.

The Testimony of Jesus

The apostle John records his overwhelming reaction to a glorious encounter with an angel:

> Then the angel said to me, "Write: 'Blessed are those who are invited to the wedding supper of the Lamb!' " And he added, "These are the true words of God." At this I fell at his feet to worship him. But he said to me, "Do not do it! I am a fellow servant with you and with your brothers who hold to the testimony of Jesus. Worship God! For the testimony of Jesus is the spirit of prophecy."
> —REVELATION 19:9-10

The revelation John was being invited to partake of came so strongly that this awesome understanding from the Spirit of Truth was too much for him. He fell down at the angel's feet to worship him. But the angel reminded John that he was just a fellow servant. All of the powerful truth the angel had stewarded was the testimony of Jesus, which they had in common with each other. Jesus' testimony is the Spirit of Prophecy.

What an awesome concept! We are invited to possess the same testimony of this angel who ministered to John. We will speak with such conviction and supernatural power, people will try to make us into idols simply because of the testimony we hold so dear.

This has happened throughout the history of the Church, even when a small portion of the testimony of Jesus was poured out on ministries. People were given roles of authority that surpassed God's intended boundaries for them, and as a result, many were disqualified.

John describes clearly this testimony:

> And this is the testimony: God has given us eternal life, and this life is in his Son. He who has the Son has life; he who does not have the Son of God does not have life.
> —1 JOHN 5:11-12

The reality of the life of Jesus in us causes everything that does not have life to react to it. For example, either people are drawn to my life, or they are angered by it.

Throughout the gospels, when Jesus entered into any situation, the Holy Spirit's presence moved through the environment, reaching out even to people He Himself did not touch. Jesus was resplendent with life, causing death and darkness to flee. He resurrected people's dead spirits by radiating His love to them.

We can do the same thing, because Christ lives in us (Romans 8:11). As His followers, we are to overflow with His life, exuding that life into the world and shining like the stars in the universe (Philippians 2:15).

These passages in Scripture are not just figurative language. Supernatural light actually comes from our very being. It may not be palpable to our natural perception, but it is an absolute reality in everyone's spiritual discernment.

> You are the light of the world . . . let your light shine before men, that they may see your good deeds and praise your Father in heaven.
> —MATTHEW 5:14-16

This light, which we are commanded to shine, illuminates even the darkest corner of the Earth with God's love. This is why it is so important for us to understand the context of Jesus' destiny; we need to learn how to operate in His love without reservation.

Once we understand that Jesus' testimony contains prophetic power twenty-four/seven, we will be unafraid to share His testimony with others. Jesus' life shines His divine nature around us, which helps us share His identity with others. When we know that no matter what we say, Jesus' life shines forth through us before we even open our mouths, evangelism seems much less daunting!

Reflection Questions

1. What does Paul's term, "the unknown God," stir in your heart? Is there an aspect of Him that remains unknown to you? Can you imagine Him wanting to reveal it to you?

2. What inspires you about Moses' desire to know God in Exodus 33-34?

3. Have you ever asked God to reveal His identity to you?

4. How have you shone like a star for Christ? What happened?

CHAPTER ELEVEN

BETROTHED AND TRANSFORMED

And he passed in front of Moses, proclaiming,
"The LORD, the LORD, the compassionate
and gracious God, slow to anger, abounding in
love and faithfulness, maintaining love to thousands,
and forgiving wickedness, rebellion and sin. Yet he does
not leave the guilty unpunished; he punishes the children
and their children for the sin of the fathers
to the third and fourth generation."
—Exodus 34:6-7

IN A MAJESTIC DECLARATION OF HIS NAME, GOD DIDN'T just pass in front of Moses. God proclaimed His virtues, attributes, and character traits. He revealed His identity. In intimate fellowship and communion, God divulged His core virtues to His servant Moses.

God used human language to define Himself. With the same mouth that spoke into existence the Heavens and the Earth, God declared the very essence of who He is. Yet speaking understandably to the hearts of men and women may have been the greater miracle!

The Promise of Divine Union

Another profound example of divine/human intimacy is found in the story of Hosea the prophet. In the book of Hosea, God describes His desire for a truly intimate and enduring relationship—to "betroth and wed" Israel as a nation. They were His covenant people. Scripture records that God said His people will no longer look at Him as master, but as husband (Hosea 2:16). He also expressed His plan to remove all idolatry from their hearts.

> I will remove the names of the Baals from her lips;
> no longer will their names be invoked.
> —HOSEA 2:17

If we pursue God as our one true love, He will remove from our lives anything or anyone we desire above Him! God promises us:

> I will betroth you to me forever;
> I will betroth you in righteousness and justice,
> In love and compassion.
> I will betroth you in faithfulness,
> And you will acknowledge the LORD.
> —HOSEA 2:19-20

God outlines six aspects of this covenant in Scripture. He will betroth us to Himself in:

1. Eternity
2. Righteousness
3. Justice
4. Love (or loving-kindness)
5. Compassion (or mercy)
6. Faithfulness

This covenant of virtues which finds its fulfillment through Jesus Christ, is similar to the virtues God identified to Moses. However, through Hosea's prophecy, God declares His marital intent. God does not merely want to employ us as servants; He wants to marry us! He wants to share His divine nature with us and bring us into perfect union with Himself. In the book of Hosea, God proclaims His wedding vows.

In 2002, I had an unusual experience that illustrates God's passion for us. In a vision, I was alone in a thick forest, waiting for God. For a long time I stood in a clearing surrounded by a thicket of trees with no apparent opening. Suddenly I heard a noise like a rampaging bear, crashing through the forest and moving toward me. Frightened, I looked for somewhere to run.

Just then, a man burst through the thicket into the clearing. It was Jesus! His eyes were on fire. As He looked into my eyes, I fell forward in the grass. I could not meet His gaze. Jesus came to me, grabbed my hand, and placed a ring on it. Then Jesus spoke to me the words found in Hosea 2:19-20. As He declared the six aspects of betrothal, I could sense that He secured each one to my soul. Jesus was so sure of my answer that He didn't ask for my assent.

Fruits of His Love

To those who desire Him simply for who He is, God wants to give Himself in marriage, sharing with them His divine character and revealing the fullness of Himself. When we allow ourselves to become fully "engaged" to Him, His divine virtues, and His identity, we begin truly to know God. As the book of Hosea declares:

> "In that day I will respond,"
>> declares the LORD
> "I will respond to the skies,
>> and they will respond to the earth;
>>> and the earth will respond to the grain,
>> the new wine and oil,
>>> and they will respond to Jezreel.
> I will plant her for myself in the land;
> I will show my love to the one I called
>> 'Not my loved one.'
> I will say to those called 'Not my people,'
>> 'You are my people';
>>> and they will say, 'You are my God.' "
>
> —Hosea 2:21-23

In Hosea 2:21-23, "grain" represents divine provision, and "new wine" represents the Holy Spirit mediating the union between us and Heaven. "Oil" represents the supernatural anointing of love in human relationships, which can inspire great healing and union among the fellowship of believers. "Jezreel" means "God plants," which represents God planting this covenant people, who are betrothed to Him, into the land to prosper. Then Hosea states that God will show love to those who were not Jesus' reward and inheritance; God will claim them for Himself, and they will claim God as their husband!

Societal Transformation

Much of the societal transformation happening in several cities around the world is a token of what occurs when men and women accept God's betrothal. The term transformation is often used to describe what transpires when an entire city is radically changed to reflect Heaven!

In these cities, salvations take place everywhere. Crime decreases almost to the point of nonexistence. Agriculture booms as the land is physically healed, and bears more fruit than is naturally possible. Every need seems to be provided for in the community. Transformation is one step beyond the Western mind-set of revival, where thousands get saved. It is when the Earth actually comes under the grace of our divine union with Jesus.

Societal transformation is God's response to our prayerful desire, inspiring the Heavens and the Earth to produce supernaturally. Where the Earth was once cursed, now it becomes blessed!

Looking for Devoted Hearts

> For the eyes of the LORD range throughout the earth to strengthen those whose hearts are fully committed to him.
> —2 CHRONICLES 16:9a

God is looking for those who recognize how awesome and worthy He is. He wants to betroth a people who are united with Him, so that we will begin to understand the unknown.

At that time, God will reveal His secret nature and show to His betrothed the fullness of His covenant.

> The LORD confides in those who fear him;
> he makes his covenant known to them.
> —PSALM 25:14

⌒ Reflection Questions ⌒

1. What aspects of God stir your desire?

2. How has God shaped you in His sixfold covenant—in eternity, righteousness, justice, loving-kindness, mercy, and faithfulness?

3. When was the last time you praised God for being worthy?

4. Read the book of Hosea; then record your thoughts and feelings on the love God has for the Church.

5. How are you responding personally to God's love?

6. How do your earthly relationships reflect your relationship with God? What do they reveal about how you are treating Him?

CHAPTER TWELVE

For Such a Time as This

*Who knows whether you have come to
the kingdom for such a time as this?*
—Esther 4:14b

ON THE EARTH, DIVINELY MANDATED EVENTS HAVE happened and will continue to happen. No one can stop or start them; they were predestined to occur. We may enter into some events with a measure of understanding, but often we get caught up in them unknowingly.

Throughout Scripture, various mandates appear in much of the Old Testament prophecy as well as in the book of Revelation. For example, Israel's restoration as a nation was a pivotal, mandated event we have witnessed during modern times.

A Divine Invitation

The story of Queen Esther, as told in Scripture, is the picture of something else altogether. Her actions to save the Jewish people during the fifth century BC represent not a mandate but a divine invitation.

Although the Jews had been free to return to Jerusalem for over fifty years, a number of Jews were still living in Babylon under Persian rule. Haman, the king's second in command, wanted to destroy the Jews. Esther was used by God to save her people from annihilation.

Growing up as an orphan, Esther probably longed for a family of her own, compensating for what she never had. Surely she longed for a godly Jewish husband to love and children to nurture. Despite her desire, though, Esther was taken to be the wife of the polygamous pagan king Ahasuerus, who ruled more than one hundred and twenty-seven provinces stretching from Ethiopia to India. Suddenly Esther joined many hundreds of women who made up the king's household.

Scripture records that the king loved Esther more than any other women, and bestowed on her great grace and favor (Esther 2:17). He made Esther queen over the land, which gave her prominence, privileges, and authority.

But even though Esther found favor with the king, hers was not a Cinderella story. She paid a price for such favor. She gave up her own desires, hoping that God would vindicate her or give her a sense of purpose in the midst of her slavery.

Esther's cousin and spiritual father, Mordecai, who was a Jewish exile and palace official, learned of a plot to kill all the Jews throughout the vast Persian kingdom. Mordecai called on Esther to go to the king and plead with him on behalf of the Jews.

> Who knows whether you have come to the kingdom for such a time as this?
>
> —ESTHER 4:14b

Nowadays many people flippantly proclaim a portion of this passage over one another, to the point that it has become a cliché in the Christian camp: "You were born for such a time as this!" But missing from the picture are the two defining words—"who knows"—that make this statement an invitation, not a mandate.

Besides the conviction of our faith, we do not have any assurance, regarding to this earthly life. God makes our life journey one that is mysterious, just as He did with Esther.

God put her in a place where she would have to make a choice that would cost her greatly either way—to risk her life to save many or to abandon many to save herself. God also put the right spiritual voice into her life to cause her to meet the challenge of taking the cup God offered.

Esther knew she risked her life by going to the king without being summoned. Mordecai, however, indicated she would die anyway since she was a Jew. If she remained silent, he reasoned, she would also miss the primary reason, purpose, and privilege in being where God had placed her.

Esther's final response indicated a growing spiritual maturity:

> Go, gather all the Jews who are present in Shushan, and fast for me; neither eat nor drink for three days, night or day. My maids and I will fast likewise. And so I will go to the king, which is against the law; and if I perish, I perish!
>
> —ESTHER 4:16

Choosing to risk everything, Esther responded to her divine invitation and embraced the cup God offered. I'm sure that Mordecai was a proud spiritual father that day!

Discerning Our Desires

Regarding the subject of invitations, many people hear encouraging words or read Scripture passages they have personally claimed. Such individuals assume that, because they desire these things to happen and because they were written or spoken, these desires are guaranteed to be fulfilled in their lifetime. This is far from true.

Each time God speaks to us, outside of the context of biblical prophecy, it is an invitation to His heart, not a predestined mandate. There is a realm of faith God must activate in us before we can enter into promises we are claiming. This is what makes it an invitation—our realm of faith is invited to be inspired by His love mingling with ours.

The good news is that God uses our desires to please Him, which in turn births a desire in us to pay the high cost in our lives. The bad news is that we can miss the invitation if we choose ourselves.

For many, this concept is extremely uncomfortable. A religious spirit confuses us into believing that, no matter how much we fail or succeed, our lot in life is the same regardless. Many people erroneously think because they have read the parable, the pay is the same for everyone; they also assume there is no way to really miss it as long as we do good works in this life.

This is the false doctrine of equality, and it permeates the Body of Christ today. We are equal in His love for us, and God is our reward. But the way we pay the daily price on Earth determines how we inherit our reward in Heaven.

Our Spiritual Inheritance

Each person's spiritual inheritance of his or her God-given position and role in Heaven is distinctive. Furthermore, each person's inheritance is reliant on how each one of us accepts God's invitation to please Him with his or her earthly life. Each inherits a spiritual investment he or she has made into eternity (Matthew 6:20).

We may all stand before God's throne with the full rights of a Christian, but our authority and role in Heaven is based on our investment in our relationship with God. He entrusts the fullness of Himself to each one who enters into Heaven, but He invites us to prepare for eternity while living on Earth. If we are faithful and obedient now, we begin to prove ourselves faithful for what we will receive in Heaven. Our storehouse there is expanded (Matthew 13:52).

At the same time, we pay a price while living on Earth, so that many can enter into divine union with God. When we come to God with a love that is not self-seeking, then great will be the way made through us. God can use such abandoned lives greatly to advance His Kingdom. All of this comes from an intimate relationship with God. Relationship is the key to authority.

Many Christian leaders have tried to bring an even playing field to all believers. Throughout the early Church, men proclaimed themselves to have the authority of the apostles, claiming to be self-appointed. Others tried to raise their teachings above Paul's, discrediting him based on his pre-Christian life. Such leaders were appointed by the people and didn't recognize that authority comes from a deep and abiding relationship with God.

It is easy to carry the weight of spiritual authority that is naturally given, but it is harder to bear the weight of authority that is based on the eyes of Heaven. Such leaders who were appointed by people had an understanding about spiritual things, but they didn't have the same equity in their relationship with God. Nor did they experience the same move of the Holy Spirit as experienced by the true apostles. No matter if they did more works or had a larger influence on bodies of believers, such leaders were not equal to the twelve apostles.

Some Christians today have presumed upon their relationship with God, proclaiming themselves to have the authority of an apostle. Often this "apostolic mantle" is bestowed by another person. Yet true spiritual authority is conferred by God and is the fruit of an intimate relationship with Him. When God confers an apostolic mantle upon us, it is backed up with spiritual power from Heaven.

Authority from Divine Favor

Many in the Church today still appoint people to church offices based on a person's ability to enact the second commandment. We appoint those who can best serve our needs, and we give them authority.

But God is looking to bestow on us a higher authority. He wants to invest His favor upon men and women who are wholeheartedly devoted to Him. Such favor will come with true spiritual authority that isn't based on church membership numbers, finances, or possessions. It is only based on a relationship with Heaven.

In the days ahead, we will see a clear distinction concerning our strategy to bear spiritual fruit. It will come in obedience to Jesus' first commandment to love God with all of our heart, mind, soul, and strength. Only as we love God with our whole heart will we see fruit born from our pursuit of His second commandment—to love others. This fruit, unlike any we have ever seen or can imagine, is an eternal treasure.

One thing is certain. While God has no favorites, there are going to be men and women who follow deeply after God's heart. These devoted ones will be the ones in whom He will invest the revelation of His Son's testimony.

☞ Reflection Questions ☜

1. What inspires you about the life of Esther?

2. What can you do now to prepare for eternity?

3. How would you describe your relationship with God? What kinds of changes can you make to grow your devotion to the Lord?

CHAPTER THIRTEEN

THE Invitation

He has made everything beautiful in its time.
He has also set eternity in the hearts of men; yet
they cannot fathom what God has done
from beginning to end.

—ECCLESIASTES 3:11

EVERYTHING I HAVE WRITTEN IN THIS BOOK HAS BEEN leading up to one question: Have you seen Heaven yet? If not, have I whet your appetite to see into the eternal realm of God and to know the hope of His calling?

Imagine thousands upon thousands of people having seen what Heaven looks like and carrying the atmosphere of Heaven in their everyday lives! It will transform communities and revive the Body of Christ.

Reflecting Our First Love

When we humble our hearts before God, desiring to know Jesus more than anything else and seeking true understanding about His inheritance—He cannot resist us. His merciful heart will melt with loving-kindness toward such passionate desire to know Him and the fellowship of His sufferings.

Heaven came to Daniel, in response to his heart cry for a greater spiritual reality:

> Do not fear, Daniel, for from the first day that you set your heart to understand, and to humble yourself before your God, your words were heard; and I have come in response to your words.
>
> —DANIEL 10:12

God's passion to share Himself with us is heralded not only throughout the Bible, but across the two thousand years since the Bible was written.

When our heart reflects an earnest passion to seek God, He responds supernaturally. We begin to walk in supernatural authority, advancing God's Kingdom daily through our intimate union with Him. We then release His life and carry His glory to the world.

An Exchange of Wills

The apostle Paul had such dynamic fulfillment and revelation in His union with Christ that God allowed him to have a thorn in his flesh.

> And lest I should be exalted above measure by the abundance of the revelations, a thorn in the flesh was given to me, a messenger of Satan to buffet me, lest I be exalted above measure. Concerning this thing I pleaded with the Lord three times that it might depart from me. And He said to me, "My grace is sufficient for you, for My strength is made perfect in weakness." Therefore most gladly I will rather boast in my infirmities, that the power of Christ may rest upon me.
>
> —2 CORINTHIANS 12:7-9

Many people have considered what his thorn in the flesh might have been. Was it health issues? Was it persecution from religious groups? Was it betrayal of relationships? Was it the politics of the day? I believe it was something far different than we might think.

Perhaps Paul's revelations and priesthood to the Lord provoked others to a spiritual hunger, and this became too much for him. The number of churches and people Paul held God-given stewardship over may have exceeded his desire and scope of influence on the Earth.

Paul's first desire was to live a quiet and simple life, fully devoted to his passion for Jesus, his highest love. But because of the great revelations and spiritual understandings that he was given from Heaven, Paul had to take an overseer's role, which he would have never chosen by his own will.

Just as we must make an exchange of our will for God's will, Paul laid down his desires to live a monastic life in intimacy with Jesus and took on a greater role in the Church. However, he did so with the right priorities in his heart.

We talked earlier about St. John of the Cross, who also reflected this passionate devotion to Jesus. He pursued a deeper union with God, which he felt was crippled by all the secondary relationships, even God-ordained ones. St. John longed to transcend this world and its desires so he could fellowship with Christ in Heaven. St. John was proof that love is a choice; it's not a feeling. He had a wonderful ministry that came only by his surrender to God's purposes.

Toward the end of his life, St. John of the Cross was put into prison for his radical faith. His friends grew greatly concerned about his welfare. Contrary to their fears, however, he was doing wonderfully. He wrote that prison was his favorite life season, because his limitations in being confined allowed him to focus solely on his holy devotion to God.

Another less-known minister in the Western world is Sundar Sadhu Singh (1889-1929). He was a Hindu priest who converted to Christianity. Sundar had an awesome ministry of healing and evangelism, but even more wonderful was his covenant and union with God. Pulled by the heart cries of sick people throughout India, Sundar actually petitioned God to give the healing mantle to someone else. He yearned for quiet days of solitude and prayer when he could devote more time to experiencing the depths of Jesus Christ.

All of these men loved ministering to God's people, but this calling was secondary to their passion for God. Much like David in Psalm 27, their heart cry was for one thing—to gaze upon the Lord in all His glory.

May it become our endeavor to resemble the saints of old, and have our passion for Jesus surpass even the greatest works we could do for God. While our ministry works are part of how we experience the divine union, they are not a substitute for it.

Responding to God's Call

For the sake of His Son, Jesus Christ, God is raising up a company of people who will be lovesick with bridal devotion. Just praying for salvation is not enough. God's standard is entering into an intimate exchange with Him, abiding in His presence.

No longer do we have the luxury to question ourselves,

"Do I hear God's voice?" In faith, we must pursue God, pressing past the shallow waters where we are only ankle deep. We must reach a place of being totally submerged in God's eternal destiny.

Up until this time in history, whatever works of Jesus that have been seen can be described by this passage:

> Indeed these are the mere edges of His ways,
>> And how small a whisper we hear of Him!
> But the thunder of His power who can understand?
>> —JOB 26:14

God is inviting us to become part of the generation that sees the testimony of Jesus thunder forth with power to the ends of the Earth. We are invited to be among the company of those who operate more fully in the supernatural realm. We are invited to bring to Jesus the fullness of His reward. We do this by seeing His full reward through the eyes of the Holy Spirit. Then, we claim these things by His divine nature, which supercedes our own limited nature.

Even today, God is revealing His name to us that was declared to the prophet Isaiah:

> Therefore My people shall know My name;
>> Therefore they shall know in that day
>>> That I am He who speaks:
> "Behold, it is I."
> How beautiful upon the mountains
>> Are the feet of him who brings good news,
>>> Who proclaims peace,
>> Who brings glad tidings of good things,
>>> Who proclaims salvation,
>> Who says to Zion,
>>> "Your God reigns!"
>>>> —ISAIAH 52:6-7

⌒Reflection Questions ⌒

1. Do you see God's hand moving in your generation? Can you describe it?

2. Have you seen Heaven yet? Is that a desire you have? If not, why?

3. Will you be one who brings the good news of Heaven to others?

4. Are you ready to be part of the throne room company? What must you do to increase the likelihood of that happening?

About the Author

FOR THE PAST DECADE, SHAWN BOLZ HAS MINISTERED with a prophetic, catalytic, and healing anointing, traveling throughout the United States and around the world. His proven track record makes Shawn a popular speaker at conferences, youth events, and revival meetings.

Currently, Shawn is on staff with WhiteDove Ministries (whitedoveministries.org), a nonprofit organization seeking to encourage people to encounter God in such a way that their lives are marked for eternity.

In 2003, Shawn launched WhiteDove's iBurn internship program (iBurn.org), through which he seeks to mentor young leaders from around the world who want to mature their ability to operate in the prophetic anointing. iBurn offers advanced leadership development for young people, 17-25 years old, by activating their spiritual calling to move in the supernatural realm.

For several years, Shawn has assisted with various national youth events such as Rock the Nations and The Call, helping to raise up a new breed of young leaders. In addition to his busy traveling schedule, Shawn serves on the staff of the International House of Prayer in Kansas City (fotb.com). As a faculty member of the Forerunner School of Ministry in Kansas City, he seeks to empower students who want to encounter God through the revelatory realm.

In addition, Shawn has been involved with numerous citywide transformation efforts, participating in conferences and regional events with organizations such as Prayer by Design (prayerby-design.com) and the Sentinel Group (sentinelgroup.org). Seeing revival spread around the world through the outpouring of the Holy Spirit is Shawn's greatest passion.

A California native, Shawn now lives with his two dogs, Maximus and Joseph, outside Kansas City, Missouri.

Engaging the Revelatory Realm of Heaven
By Paul Keith Davis

An ocean of divine truth is waiting to be discovered.
In this fascinating book, Paul Keith Davis reveals how those
anointed with the Spirits of Wisdom and Revelation will see an
awesome demonstration of God's glory in the coming days.
Retail: $12

Available online at www.streamsministries.com
Or by calling 1-888-441-8080

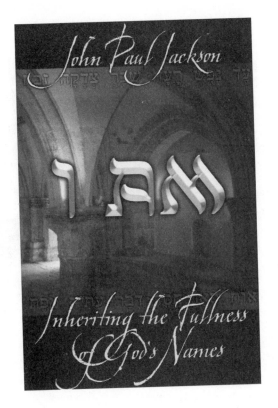

I AM: Inheriting the Fullness of God's Names
By John Paul Jackson

As the richly dowried children of God, we are heirs to
God's abundant resources and wealth. Today, as well as
throughout eternity, we can reap the amazing blessings of
greater influence, favor, and protection that come with God's
name. By the mere power of His name, all healing springs
forth, all provisions flow, and all authority is conferred.
As you embark on the glorious adventure of knowing God,
let Him show you the amazing mysteries and wonders
reserved for those who bear His name.
Retail: $10

Available online at www.streamsministries.com
Or by calling 1-888-441-8080

I AM: 365 Names of God
By John Paul Jackson

Designed for daily reading and meditation,
John Paul Jackson has collected 365 names of God that will
guide you into becoming a person who consistently abides
in God's presence. God's names are a disclosure of God
Himself. In His name, there is peace, comfort, provision,
healing, and destiny. When you meditate on a name of God,
you will discover His transforming power. Hardback.

Retail: $24

Available online at www.streamsministries.com
Or by calling 1-888-441-8080